A Steadfast Heart

Madison Otto

A Steadfast Heart

Madison Otto

A Steadfast Heart
Copyright © 2016 by Madison Otto

Printed in the United States of America.
Design, editing, and production: Steve Lewis
ISBN: 978-0-9974267-1-7
Library of Congress Control Number: 2016961023

Published by Eagle Trail Press Box 3671 Parker, Colorado 80134
info@EagleTrailPress.com

Introduction

I love to journal. I have lots of journals. A lot of times I would record when I finally understood something I never understood before. Maybe it was something my Bible Study teacher said or an answered prayer. There's always been this thought in the back of my mind that I think the Lord put there.

"You're going to publish your journal some day."

"Yeah, okay God. We'll see."

"When you're 21."

"Hmm, sure, that'd be cool. I've always wanted to write a book. But we'll see how that plays out."

Through various circumstances and lots of prayer and counsel I kept getting green lights and 'go-for-its' over and over again.

"Okay, God, I got Your message! I'll do it. Let's see what You want to do."

Never underestimate how clear the Lord is when He has a task for you. If you feel like He is giving you a nudge, obey! He'll take it from there.

For many years I thought, "I don't have a testimony." I grew up in a Christian home, had a sheltered childhood, and have none of those experiences like other people's incredible, give-you-goosebumps testimonies. It wasn't until I started going to cosmetology school that the Lord started showing me what my testimony is. And this is it: *The Lord is good.*

I am His daughter. A princess. Redeemed. Adopted. Made holy and blameless. This is who I am.

As a child I was bossy and selfish and I am not proud of who I was when I was little. I vaguely remember bits and pieces but I remember the story my parents told me of what happened. I was about 7-years old when the Lord moved me. I had made an altar in my room and cried all day. When my parents asked what was wrong I told them that God told me I was being a bad girl.

Since that day my parents said they could see a change had happened in my heart. I know that something changed. My life began to be "Christian because it's what I want to be" not just because it's what my family is. But not until I was about 13 did my attitude turn from "this is just what you do" to falling in love with the One who had saved my heart. Since then, the Lord has opened so many doors and offered so many opportunities in my life. I love to talk about what He has done.

As my high school graduation was looming ahead, I began to pray about what He would want me to do next. I never had a desire to go to college. Even if I did, what would I study? I always had an interest in hair and nails and facials. My friends always said, "You should do this for a living!" Hmm, that was a thought. I always wanted to be a missionary, but I never felt led to go anywhere. "What are You doing, God? If I'm going to be a missionary You're going to have to tell me where to go!" But nothing came to me. Okay, so I was stuck wondering what to do. I kept hearing 'grow where you're planted' and 'minister to the people next door'. Ooh! I gotcha! I'm supposed to be a missionary to my local mission field. Here, where I live! I already know the language and culture, now I just have to get out there.

All right, cosmetology. I had an interest and a talent (so I was told) and it fit everything I liked. I get my hands into the hair of willing models (not just reluctant sisters) and meet all kinds of new people and I like to talk and listen. It was perfect. Then, I came to the point when I realized that I didn't know how to be a missionary. What does a missionary do? As I prayed about this I came across 1 John 2:6, "The one who says he abides in Him ought himself to walk in the same manner as He walked."

But what does that mean? So I began to look at how Jesus interacted with the crowds while He walked on earth. Then I saw it! He didn't point His finger at anyone. He didn't tell them that He couldn't hang out with "their kind" until they changed. He didn't participate in their lifestyle but He loved them. He even looked at the Pharisees and the Romans with love. He waited until they came to Him.

"Live as He lived" is what the passage said. Okay, I just needed to obey His commandments and He would work in my obedience. My life would be a witness of how good He is, and hopefully the people around me would see His love in me, as impossible as that seems. He is the God of the impossible and He truly does use the obedient.

My mission: Break the 'stereotype Christian' view. How? By simply being who the Lord made me to be and being obedient to how He has asked me to live. He is good, you guys!

And that's exactly it! That's all there is to it. The Lord has never given us reason to doubt. He is good!

Madison

1

Dear Reader,

In the following pages you will be reading the thoughts and prayers of a pre-teen girl. Sometimes a young girl's mind can seem to be all over the place, and at other times it is fixated on something specific. My hope is that in reading you can relate to how a young girl thinks, perhaps your daughter or sister or even yourself. Or maybe it will strike a memory of how you saw things when you were that age. I hope that in sharing this story of how I grew close to God by intentionally focusing on Him in a tumultuous stage of life, you too will find creative ways to intentionally include Him in your days. Invite Jesus into your thoughts, all thoughts, and "He will make your paths straight" (Proverbs 3:6).

8-27-07

Hi! My name is Maddie and I'm 12½. I'm in 7th grade and I have 3 siblings and I'm homeschooled! I have been homeschooled since Kindergarten. My dad is a chiropractor and we live in Parker, Colorado. We go to a church called The Mountain. It's great! Bonus, everyone in the church is homeschooled! We also have friends that live a mile and a half up the hill in the neighborhood and we feel like cousins! We see them almost every day. It's great! Nate is the boy, and Louisa is the girl. Nate is my brother Noah's age, 10½. Lou is 8½ and she plays with my sisters Morgan, 6 and Claire, 3½. The Blake family (that's their last name) want to adopt. They have a foster child right now and his name is Benjamin. He's 2 years old. And there's the Reinhart family (more friends)! Hannah and Adam are 12½, they're twins! Caroline is 10½ and Abby is 5½.

Today we were at the Gensen's house all day (more friends). Emily is 16, Diana 14, Molly 9, Sarah 2 and Mrs. Gensen is pregnant! Anyway, we were canning peaches all day and YUM they're goooood! I love peaches.

8-29-07

Hi! It's me again, did you know me and Noah are black belts in Tae Kwon Do? I play piano too. The Reinharts are moving to 40 acres of land with an inground pool and an indoor arena and a barn. So sweet! Back to piano, I'm teaching my mom a certain song that's a duet. It's fun! I love worship dance too if you didn't know.

9-2-07

The sermon at church today was about, well… complaining and arguing. The quote was funny!

Ahem… "Let's be shiners not whiners." I thought it was hilarious! Good night!

9-3-07

Today is Labor Day and we stayed home all day. I did a lot of studying on hermit crabs today. I told you I was getting 2 right? I love hermit crabs.

9-4-07

It's almost 11pm and my nails are still a little bit wet (I painted my nails). I'm here in bed waiting for Mama to come tell me good night. Nate and Lou came to play today, we rode our bikes up to their house and they rode back with us. We did the same taking them home except… I nearly ran over a baby bull snake! I wasn't paying attention and I was looking down, so I was going along and all of a sudden I saw it almost under my tire. I screamed! It scared me to see it all of a sudden like that. Anyway it was a snake adventure. We did school today too. Duh.

9-6-07

Guess what I just figured out! I already have a container for my hermit crabs! But there's a problem, I have nowhere to put it. I'll just have to talk to Mama tomorrow. Tomorrow is the first day of

Succoth (it's a Jewish holiday). We're studying it for school, seeing what it's like and to do that we have to make a fort called a sukka. We have to hang fruit from the ceiling too. Then we'll have the Blakes over for dinner to study the holiday with us. It goes for a whole week.

I'm just here dreaming about... hermit crabs. Ahh, so cute. Okay, okay, they're not that cute but you've got to admit they're sort of cute. But they're extremely fun and interesting and safe and social and lovable. I love them. I might actually get 4 crabs. But I might not. I need to talk to Mama first. I love hermys.

9-7-07

Today was the first day of Succoth. We also finished our sukka today. We used our deck for most of it, we tied sticks to the railing and tied strings from the door and tied the fruit on it. Then we put a picnic rug out and chairs and a table. Later we cut sunflowers to weave in between the railings and the sticks. They were beautiful after we were finished but now they're dry. The Blakes came over and we had the feast and did the Bible reading and lit candles. AWANA starts in 2 days. I'm too old to do it now, so Daddy is going to take me on a date-ish thing. He's taking me to dinner and maybe to a store. It'll be fun!

9-8-07

Me and Mom went shopping today. We went to

a whole bunch of stores and we had a blast! When we got home and it got dark out, gnats invaded our house. It was disgusting. Then Mom came up with this marvelous invention… duct tape gnat stickers! It worked great! We just put duct tape on my lights and POOF! half of the gnats were gone. Amazing huh? Yeah, I thought so too. Dad told me I need to write him a 2-page report on hermit crabs.

9-9-07

This was the first day of AWANA. I wasn't going to teach this year but there are so many kids. So Mom and Dad are going to talk about it.

9-11-07

Today was the 6th anniversary of the Twin Towers collapsing.

9-12-07

I'm sad because my FUN summer is gone, forever. Today was the first day that we had EVERYTHING going on. We went to Spanish, piano, Tae Kwon Do and I had school and I finished my report for Dad today. He loves it. I'm so sleepy right now. I went to bed at midnight last night, and the night before that, and you know what time it is now? Uh huh, midnight. Well, almost.

9-15-07

I went to the Reinhart's new house (the one with the pool) today! I got up at 10am this morning and got a chance to sleepover at the Reinhart's tonight. I read 20 pages of my Bible tonight so I don't have to read it tomorrow night (it's going to be a late night). Caroline thinks hermit crabs are "Ew! Gross! Yuck!" Hannah said she thinks they're alright. I love hermit crabs. Tomorrow is Sunday and me and Dad are going out during AWANA. I wonder who is helping in the Cubbies.

9-20-07

I had such a wonderful day! This is how it all started... I got up this morning and no one else was up yet. Dad had already gone to work and Mama was still in her room so I did my school work and most of my chores when the phone rang. It was Mrs. Blake. After a while my mom told me to get the other kids up because Mrs. B asked us if we wanted to come see their new house! They haven't moved yet but it's beautiful! It's 80 acres. We explored some of it and discovered that you can soften your hands by taking the grain off the grass in your hands and rubbing it in your palms then let it fly away. Their barn is going to be finished to be a school room/office on one side and a real barn on the other side for their chickens and goats and other animals. It's a gorgeous place to live. After we got home we went for a walk and picked some flowers for our flower press. The sunset changed color so many times tonight! I love sunsets.

9-23-07

Today is Sunday and I was a Cubbies helper. The other helper couldn't come. I had a blast!

9-25-07

We went shopping today! We went to Big Lots, Lemstone, Walmart, the bank, and PetSmart. There's a stupid fly buzzing around my room right now and I'm going downstairs to get the fly swatter and chase it down. Fee-fi-fo-fum, beware fly! Nate gave me some of his extra hermit crab stuff. I love the Blakes!

9-28-07

Tomorrow! Tomorrow we're leaving for Steamboat Springs! It's a 4-hour drive but it's worth it. We took Daddy out to see the Blake's new house this afternoon. After that Dad and Noah took us shooting! Noah let me shoot his shotgun. Out of about 20 shots I hit 3 clays the whole time. Pretty good huh? I have to go to bed, Dad wants to get to Steamboat by 3pm. After we get home I can get my crabbys!

9-29-07

Four hours of driving today, but so worth it. It's raining right now, I hope it stops by morning. Dad says we might go on a bike ride tomorrow. Me and Claire are sharing a bed, and Noah and Morgan get the fold-out couch, Mom and Dad get the master bedroom. We watched 'Man from…'? I don't remember. But I liked it. I'm looking forward to the rest of vacation.

10-2-07

We had an awesome lunch today. I had to babysit my siblings in the morning and we didn't get along very well. Mama says I might start Precept studies with her this year. But we need to pray about it first. One day closer to getting my crabs!

10-5-07

Vacation is over. Boohoo. I'm sad but I'll be glad to be home again. Mama says she sees a hint of green in my hair. Not again! Ugh. Chlorine turns my hair green. We went on a hike today, and at the end of the trail WAS A WATERFALL! It was beautiful. We went to a museum today too. It was so cool. They had a 1869 square grand piano that was brought over the mountains in a covered wagon and I got to play Fur Elise on it! When we got back we went on a bike ride and rode past the sulfur springs. Yuck! It smells like eggs. Blek.

10-6-07

I DID A DIVE OFF THE BOARD FOR THE FIRST TIME! AND ON THE LAST DAY OF VACATION AND PROBABLY MY LAST CHANCE TOO! I'm so happy!

10-8-07

Tomorrow's the possible big day! Mama says we'll have to see how the day goes. Oh! I hope! I hope! I hope!

10-9-07

I got my crabs today! And I saw one the size of an M'n'M and Mama said I could get it tomorrow. Nate got to come with us today to help me pick them out. They're so cute! I named them Sampson and Delilah. I'm gonna name the one I'm getting, tomorrow Anna. If you haven't noticed, I've named my crabs Bible names. They love the coconut in their crabbitat. I love them so much! XOXoxOxOXo

10-10-07

First thing, we (me, Mama and Claire) went to the dentist for a cleaning. I have two cavities. One tiny one and one they're watching. Speaking of tiny I couldn't find the tiny crab today. Instead I got one that I thought was the tiny one but I thought maybe it was too big but I got it anyway. Two actually. Two crabs. I got one smaller than the other, which I named Joshua, and the second I named Sarah. And I thought I killed her, but she's molting. She will not come out of her shell no matter what. I found her in some dirt (she buried herself) and that's a sign of molting. And that's when you're NEVER supposed to bathe a crab or move it or mess with it. I pretty much did everything you're not supposed to do with a molting crab before I knew she was even molting. I might exchange her if she doesn't molt safely. I wish I bought that tiny one yesterday.

10-11-07

Sarah still won't come out. I took home a molting crab. I'm going to exchange her. It's sad I think. The other crabs are all healthy. During Bible study today me, Noah and Nate hung out with the crabs and listened to 'Hank the Cow Dog'. I love Hank the Cow Dog. Tomorrow the Blakes are coming over for

Rah Sha Shana, a Jewish feast, for school. Me and Noah have bow testing at Tae Kwon Do tomorrow. I think crabs are so much fun, don't you? I love my hermit crabs.

10-12-07

I got to meet the one and only Bill Superfoot! He's the guy that can only kick with one leg and trained it to be faster than average speed. I think me and Noah passed our test, but there are a few things I need to work on.

10-13-07

First thing today Mama went out to PetSmart and exchanged the crab and yes it was dead. Sadly. After that Mama got me a vanilla steamer and she got a vanilla chai. From there we went to Beautiful Girlhood and had so much fun there. Because for one, it's already fun. And two, afterward almost all the girls wanted to know about hermit crabs. I felt really smart.

10-14-07

My favorite part of the day was having a long conversation with Aika. She's a Japanese girl who came to America to learn worship dance then go back and teach it in Japan. She doesn't speak English very well but she has an electric translator. Tomorrow is the day we get to go to the Museum for the Titanic exhibit. And we need to leave here just after 7am and drop Claire off at a friend's house. I need to get to sleep so good night. Oh! My new crab Sarah is doing really well and she's really brave. I love her.

10-15-07

The Titanic exhibit was so cool! We were each given cards with names of passengers who were on the Titanic, so it was like we were those people, and we got to see if our person survived or not. My ticket said I was Mrs. Helene Baxter from Canada. I survived! There was even a piece of the Titanic in a box and I got to touch it! We car pooled with the Blakes and we had so much fun. We went to the IMAX and I loved it!

10-17-07

I still have lots of my Bible study homework left. I'm halfway through Day 2. There are different days in Precepts. At piano today I got a $5 gift card, which means I got 100 piano bucks, each buck for a day I practiced. My teacher Mrs. VanScoyk found a song called 'The Hermit Crab Cha Cha'. Cool huh? I'm going to learn it. Tomorrow I have my first Bible study and then right after that I have to go babysit Dylon across the street. I'll be there until 10pm so I can take my Bible study over there and work on it.

10-18-07

Something bit me today! I was in Noah's room just lying there and all of a sudden it felt like a needle was going through my lip. It left a white and red mark where it bit me. We looked for whatever it was but couldn't find it. Great, it's still out there somewhere. Anyway I think it was a wasp, NOT a spider because- oh never mind. Well, I think it was a wasp because we sometimes have wasps in our house. I had my first Bible Study today. And it is sooo much fun! Then I babysat Dylon and that was fun.

10-19-07

The Reinharts asked me to sleepover tonight and Mama said yes! Imagine that! They're doing Beautiful Girlhood with us too! So they're gonna take me to Beautiful Girlhood in the morning.

10-20-07

I have a new favorite tea. Vanilla Hazelnut with honey. YUM. I finished my Bible study for this week with the Reinharts. I love the Reinharts. We went to Beautiful Girlhood together today. I loved today.

10-21-07

SNOW!!!!! I LOVE SNOW!!!!! I woke up to a few inches on the ground today. I'm so extremely tired tonight. I need sleep. I love sleep. I love tea too. And crabs. And friends. And Precept studies. Good night.

10-23-07

I got to see Sarah change shells tonight! Twice! Amazing. Us kids had so much fun at the Reinharts today. They still had a little snow left and they had some of a sledding ramp left. We built onto it and made it HUGE. When the boys went off it they went about 4 or 5 feet off the ground. Funny to watch! I NEED sleep! I have a headache and I need sleep NOW! Oh! Grandma is coming in 2 days so Mama had me do triple the school work today because we skipped school yesterday and we need to get ahead for when Grandma gets here. I love Grandma, and sledding, and friends. Oh! And my family and most importantly my God and Savior Jesus Christ.

10-29-07

Grandma left today. Boohoo! We got our sidewalk poured today. And our dishwasher broke. So me and Noah have to hand wash the dishes.

10-31-07

Dad is now 41 years old. Happy birthday Dad! I think last year's harvest party was so much more fun. I'm not complaining, I'm just saying last year's fest was more fun.

11-2-07

Did I forget to tell you that I got to go to a birthday party in 1802? We crocheted and churned butter and collected eggs and bobbed for apples and milked a cardboard cow. They hid baby bottles behind it and we milked the bottles. I had SOOO much fun!

11-3-07

The Reinharts took me to Beautiful Girlhood. The session was so good. It was about Ideals, Ambitions, Purpose, and Dreams. We each got sheets that had questions on them about what our ambitions are. I wrote that I want to be an author, and a mom. I want to be a godly woman, honest and kind, trustworthy and hardworking. I want to be a good example to my neighbors and the people who look up to me. And I want to remember the quote of the day, it was so good!

"So it is imperative that a girl set before her good and pure ideals, that she sets her mark high. It is better to aim at the impossible than to be content with the inferior."

We need to set back the clocks tonight.

11-4-07

My most favorite part of my day was probably spending time with Aika (the Japanese girl). I gave her a gift box thing (made for cookies) and put 4 cookies and some candy in it and guess what! Before I gave her the gift she gave me a gift! Japanese snacks. Yum! She liked her gift too. We took the Blakes to AWANA tonight. I helped in Cubbies again. We had fun. The Blakes are almost all the way packed. They move Saturday.

11-5-07

They got their match! The Blakes know who their second foster baby is gonna be! They're getting a baby girl, in one week. She's going to be 2 weeks old! I can't wait! Mama went shopping for Mrs. Blake and got some awesome stuff. I'm so excited!

11-6-07

We get to see the baby tomorrow! They aren't bringing her home until after they move which is in 4 days. I can't wait! I'm making 2 blankets (crochet of course), one for Benjamin, and Mama got me some baby soft yarn to make the baby's. I've made all of Benjamin's squares today. All 16 of them! All I need to do is sew them together. Then I'll start the baby's. Her colors are lavender and white. I love crocheting!

11-7-07

She is the most precious thing I have seen in a long, long, LONG time. Her feet are as long as my finger. I finished Benjamin's blanket today. And have a couple squares done for the baby's. Oh! Mama said Mrs. Blake said they're probably going to name her Rachel Mae. Two more days till the Blakes move and Grandma Linda comes! The baby is sooo cute! I love her.

11-8-07

No more hand washing dishes! The dishwasher people came and fixed it. We are spoiled aren't we? We have so many machines that do things for us. It was God's plan to have dishwashers invented so I thank and praise Him for them! And for everything else He has done for us. We finished the book of Genesis today at Bible Study. We're gonna start Revelation next. I'm excited! Grandma is coming in two days! And the Blakes are moving that day too. Daddy brought home the movie Ratatouille and we watched it tonight.

11-12-07

I can't wait till tomorrow! The Blakes get the baby, Rachel. We went to the pool today! There were a lot of people there. We're going to the Lone Tree pool tomorrow.

11-16-07

Grandma Linda is gone. She went home. She left yesterday but before she left we got 6 skeins of yarn to make Christmas gifts. I already rolled them into balls. We also had small group last night and I got to hold Rachel and I got to feed her a bottle, twice! And then played knock-out (basketball) with the boys. We went to see the Bee Movie with Nate and Lou yesterday. I liked it.

2

S ince the previous journal was written Noah
and I tested for our second degree black belts
in Tae Kwon Do. And in the summer of 2008 my
family bought land, we call it the property, 30 minutes from where we live. There is an old homestead
on the property that has ponds and the neighbor's
cattle were grazing the pasture there. We needed to
build new fences and tear down old ones. We spent
many, many days out there, and I couldn't be more
grateful for it. This particular journal was written
in the "Elsie Dinsmore Life of Faith" journal and
during the writing of this journal I was learning how
to work hard. To do things right the first time and
to not stop until the job is finished and well done. I

gained a strong work ethic and it has served me well ever since.

October 6, 2008

I have been waiting for this book for SO long! And today it came in the mail! Actually I've only been waiting a week and six days. I love the Elsie books. I'm already on Book 5! They're so good!

This section says this is where to write my dreams. My dream is to someday become an author. And a homeschooling mom. God, help me to accomplish my dreams. Your will be done and we'll give You the praise.

1 Corinthians 13:4-5

"Love is patient, love is kind, it does not boast, it isn't selfish, it does not covet, it is not rude..." I hope I can memorize the rest soon.

October 7, 2008

Tonight was such a great night. I got to go to Kirren's AWANA festival and I got to help run a booth (the penny toss). And I was chased by a man with a wet sponge. Actually I deserved it. I was teasing him and trying to spray him with canned whipped cream. And I won a raffle! Four Laura Ingles books.

Yesterday, our dog Allie attacked our little dog Meg. Meg has two puncture wounds and the vet had to put staples in her neck. I pray that she gets better really soon.

Answer to prayer on October 7th. Thank You, Lord that our dog Meg is doing so much better! We praise You.

October 8, 2008

I have a dentist appointment today. Drilling and shots. :'(

Today, Lord, please help all to go well at the dentist and that I don't feel the shots or flinch. Thank You for always being there for me.

Weak areas in my life: Respect, patience, and holding my tongue. Dear Helper of All, help me to realize what I am thinking before I speak. I want to be respectful and patient. But I can't do it alone, I need You to help me. Amen.

October 10, 2008

Lord, please help us stay warm at the property today. I also pray that nobody gets hurt while working out there today, please. And be with the Blake family and with Rachel's adoption case. Amen.

It's cold out today and we need to build fence. I just hope the girls will stay warm. I wish it would snow sometime soon.

P.M. We stayed warm! We are hoping that we can finish the fence tomorrow. After we were on our way home Daddy told me, "You did really good today. Very helpful." I felt so special and proud. When we got back, Claire was in the shower and I told her it was time to get out and said, "Aren't you done yet?" Her response, "I'm doing the one after the beginning! The last one." Meaning conditioner, after the shampoo. It was funny. I finished the 5th Elsie Book today. It was good!

I am having a really hard time with patience and respect and controlling my anger. I get angry when my parents ask me to do something and I get confused when they ask me to change what I'm doing, that makes me angry too. Help me control my anger!

October 11, 2008

We had church today and had AWANA tonight. Dad took me to the mystery store tonight. He's been telling me he's going to take me somewhere fun and special but wouldn't tell me where. It was Bass Pro! Of course, I had my suspicions. I love that store.

I'm tired and I still have to shower and it's getting cold sitting here. Good night.

October 12, 2008

Lord, I pray that You can help me stay fully awake today. I went to bed late and got up early. Thanks, Amen.

October 15, 2008

Dance was today and we learned a LOT of our dance. It was great! The Reinharts are leaving tomorrow for a wedding in Florida. It's for Mrs. R's sister. I'm glad but bummed too. I'm gonna miss them. Mrs. R is one of the bridesmaids and Abby is the flower girl. I only have half of a chapter left in the 6th Elsie Book.

October 16, 2008

The other day I found a prophecy in Isaiah 9:6! "A child will be born." It is also found in Luke. I was really happy and excited!

October 17, 2008

We're going to finish building the fence today.

P.M. We finished the fence but we still have the gates to do. I'm in the second chapter of the 7th Elsie Book. I have to babysit the girls all day tomorrow. And I have to play 3 hours of piano. Ugh.

Trial: I'm moody and I have an attitude. I am trying to learn how to control it. Lord, help me!

I don't feel so good right now. My stomach feels icky and uncomfortable. Please take away my discomfort. And please Father, help me with my attitude and my moods. Thank You, Amen.

October 19, 2008

There wasn't any AWANA tonight so Daddy declared a movie night! We watched "The Incredibles" and Claire fell asleep buried in my lap.

October 21, 2008

We did a lot of school work today. I found out that I'm sleeping over at Kirren's house on Friday! Yay! Claire and I have dance tomorrow! Yay again! It rained some today and it's raining again now! Yay again! Lord, be with us all tonight, help us sleep well without troublesome thoughts. Amen.

October 22, 2008

I had dance today. And I got the cardboard for my Pompeii model. We got snow today. Whoo hoo! Tonight Morgan prayed that the Blake's dogs won't get out and meet any porcupines or skunks.

I'm 75 pages behind in one of my school books. I'm sad. Tomorrow we have co-op with the Blakes and have writing and science class and I'm gonna make my Pompeii model.

Lord, help me to be instantly obedient. And help me with my respect. Amen.

Yep, that's my prayer. Although I think it's partially my hormones. But I'm getting better in my weak spots. :)

October 23, 2008

The Headricks are friends that are more like family. Us kids have grown up together. They moved away for a while but when they moved back we were just as close as ever!

Dad and Noah are getting ready to go hunting with David and Briggham Headrick in South Dakota. I made my Pompeii today out of a bottle and dirt, I'm gonna test it tonight when Daddy gets home. We had co-op and we frosted the planet cookies. Oh! I almost forgot, I whopped Noah and Nate at Mayhem (the shooting game)! And they both admitted that I beat them by far every time!

October 24, 2008

It has been an amazing day! Noah and Dad left

this morning, then I was busy doing chores, practiced piano, watched King George and the Ducky (Veggie Tales), and wrote a report on Pompeii. Kirren came and took me to a book fair at her school. It was pretty cool. I bought 'Eve of the Emperor Penguin'. That's a Magic Tree House book. And I bought 'Marley', a dog book for Noah. 'Dogerella' for Morgan and a Christmas Dora book for Claire.

When we got to Kirren's house I was put into a hotel. Kirren turned the spare room into a hotel with the stationary and the Bible and even a key to my room! She taped a folded piece of paper to the door and put a hole with a red dot in it so that when I slide my key into it and it looks green like it's unlocked. Isn't that clever? We made brownies and did a craft, then painted nails and watched "Anne of Green Gables." It's past midnight now and Rachel's 1st birthday is tomorrow.

October 25, 2008

Another amazing day! (I say matter of factly)

We fell asleep around 1am this morning and got up at 8am then watched some of the 3rd Anne of Green Gables movie. We played Webkinz after that. Mrs. Siewert took us girls to a "Schoolhouse Rocks" play. It was good. I mean, very enjoyable. After Mrs. Siewert took us home we played Webkinz again. Mama picked me up and we went to Rachel Mae's 1st birthday party! She's one year old! Unbelievable!

Nate and I watched more of the 3rd Anne movie
but now we're home and Noah called... Brigg shot
an animal (unknown species) and everybody got
nicknames while they're up there. Brigg is 'Alice'.
David is 'Starbucks'. Noah is 'Gomer'. And Dad is
'Grandma'. Isn't that funny? Mama is letting all of us
girls sleep in her bed tonight.

October 26, 2008

Thank You, Lord, for giving me such a WON-
DERFUL family! I don't know what I would do
without them. And with Your grace we will shine
Your glory through our words, actions and prayers.

October 27, 2008

I watched a little more of the 3rd Anne movie
while everybody was at Tae Kwon Do. It was a little
disturbing alone. Watching it with Mom or some-
body would be okay, but NOT alone. It's very tragic.
I had a piano lesson today and Mrs. French said,
"I'm strict because I want you to be a professional
pianist." Can you believe it!?

Tonight during family worship and study Claire
volunteered to pray for all of us. Morgan's prayer
request was that the Blake's dogs wouldn't meet
any porcupines so Claire prayed, "Dear God, don't
let the Blake's dogs run into any trees, porcupines,
skunks, elk, moose, squirrels, coyotes..." She went on
and on, we were all trying to control our laughter,
it was so funny! After she was finished I said to her,
"You forgot about buffaloes." Claire said, "Oh! And

help the dogs not meet any buffalo. Amen." I wanted to remember that.

Later: I can't sleep so I'm writing. I need LOTS of patience with my sisters right now. Lord, give me patience. I love You, Amen.

October 28, 2008

The Reinharts got back from the wedding today and came to pick up their animals. We were watching the hamsters and the fish. Hannah brought me something from Florida. A sand dollar! I broke it even before I knew what was in that little bag. But that's okay because Mom showed me the little doves inside. It's so pretty! Tomorrow is observation day at dance! It's when parents come to watch the class. It's going to be a GREAT day!

October 30, 2008

This morning when I got up I looked out the window and the sun was just coming up and there were rays on the ground. It gave me a thrill, how romantic.

October 31, 2008

What a marvelous day! We got a lot done at the property today. There's one more gate to put up, then Dad and Noah will be done building the fence. Mom and I cleaned out more debris from under the floor in the homestead and we dumped it in the cistern and filled it almost four feet higher!

The Harvest party was fabulous. We had dancing and my game booth (fishing for candy) was everybody's favorite. We're going to the property again tomorrow.

Oh! I forgot two things! One: It's Dad's birthday! Two: Diana Gensen was my dance partner at the party tonight. She was the boy, and she so flattered me!

I was reading Psalm 136 and it says "His love endures forever" 26 times! His love DOES endure FOREVER! What a marvelous God we serve! For a long time I have wanted to make a list of who God is to me.

Yahweh, Great Counselor, The One, Comforter, Healer, Listener, Creator, I AM, Lover of all, King, Who is, Who was, Who is to come, Great Protector, Almighty, Listener, Jesus.

November 1, 2008

I forgot to tell you that I found out we're leaving for vacation THIS Friday! That's only 6 days!

We got a lot done at the property today and guess what?! We got home at 4:30pm, with everything on our list finished! That's a big deal, that never happens. The time change is tonight.

November 2, 2008

Only 3 days ago I wrote that I had read Psalm 136 "His love endures forever." Today at church we sang that very thing! What a coincidence!

November 3, 2008

We had a busy day. We hooked the lawn mower

to its trailer and picked up the yard so I can mow without running over rocks and busting the blades. It took over 3 trips to unload the trailer from all the stuff in the yard. Noah mowed for the first time by himself today. I need a shower, so good night! The time change is really making me tired.

November 4, 2008

Election Day. Obama won. But that's a wonderful thing because God wanted him to be president. I don't know why but okay God. I pray for Obama. I pray You will lay Your hand upon his heart and maybe, God, the Bible will be taught in public schools again. And people will come to You for everything. Do Your will Lord, I know it is the best. In Jesus' name, Amen.

November 5, 2008

TWO MORE DAYS UNTIL WE LEAVE! Can't you tell I'm excited? For vacation we're going to Kentucky this year. All we have is tomorrow and the next morning we leave the house before 7:30am! We're gonna have SO much fun!

November 7, 2008

Lord, Thank You for keeping us safe on this incredibly fun trip. The plane ride was really fun. We had a bobcat on the tail of our plane. They had TVs on the headrests! Our rental car is red. It's some kind of minivan with a squarish back. For dinner we went to a cute little-bitty restaurant and there was nobody there but us. It's only 7:00pm here in Kentucky. It's

6:00pm at home but it feels like at least 9:30 after a long day of traveling. Oh! I've been to 2 new states today! Tennessee and Kentucky.

November 8, 2008

What a tremendously busy day. Mama got us up at almost 9:00am. Claire is sharing my bed with me tonight, Morgan was with me last night. After breakfast we went to Walmart and there were some Amish people shopping there too!

We played at the swing set across the street. The trees are so beautiful here! We're going to a concert later tonight in Nashville. The Grand Ole Opry with Randy Travis and Craig Morgan and a whole bunch of other guys! All country music!

November 9, 2008

After last night I've promised myself that I'm never going to live in a big city. The air was too smokey.

The music was LOUD at the Opry. But I had a BLAST! We got home at 1:00am and I finally got in bed at 2:00am. On the way to the Opry we stopped at an old, old cemetery. The sign said, "Dedicated to the soldiers buried here." There were stones that said from the Revolutionary War, Civil War, Mexican War, War of 1812, and most of the headstones were so old we couldn't read them. And we saw two that said, 'Born in 1790'. It was SO cool! We hung out today. Dad bought Kung Fu Panda, so we're gonna watch it tonight. We're going to the Creation Museum tomorrow. WHOO HOO!

November 10, 2008

What an incredibly fascinating, unbelievably fun, awesome day! I was up at about 5:30am Colorado time. In the car Mama read 'Man of the Family' by Ralph Moody (one of our favorites!) and I fell asleep! That NEVER happens. We went to the museum and there were a lot of fun and fascinating things. And a lot of sad things too, like the Fall and the Flood. They were brought to life to me. Then there were some dinosaurs that sort of freaked me out. God is SOOO amazing and creative! Dad got us a pumpkin and vanilla swirl ice cream after lunch. Then we went to this booth for an observatory show and we gave our tickets to the lady and she said, "So you're a half an hour late." "What?" "It's 2:15." "Oh! We're on the wrong time zone!" We were on 1:15! The museum was just on the other side of the time divide. It was funny. On our way out of the museum we went to the gift shop and I got postcards for my friends and I got a bookmark with strings! What a wonderful day!

Lord, I am struggling with getting along with my siblings. Especially with my words. Father, I need Your grace and Your help to accomplish this goal to help us get along and glorify You. I praise You for everything You do. I love You. Amen.

November, 11, 2008

Another great day! The horse farms were AMAZ-

ING! So many famous (nationwide and worldwide) horses and places. We drove around with a guide and she told us all about the things we were seeing as we drove by. She reminded both Noah and me of our Grandma Otto. AND we stopped at the farm where Secretariat was buried! We saw his grave! Did you know that for famous race horses, when they die only their head, hooves, and heart are buried? That's because it's the head, hooves, and heart that make a race horse great. It was so cool! We're almost home (back to the condo) now. Dad said it's a pizza/cookie/movie night.

I've noticed that all of us siblings—especially me—aren't very nice to each other. Lord, I need Your most efficient help, grace, and love to overcome this habit. Amen.

November 12, 2008

We went to Mammoth Cave today! It was SO cool. We got to see the frozen Niagara too! It was HUGE and so pretty. Now I'm a 'Junior Park Ranger'.

I had fun. Tomorrow is our last day of vacation. :(But I miss Colorado. We're going to watch 'Kit Kittredge' tonight (I think. I hope.)

I think I am the most fortunate girl ever! To have a family like mine, and being able to do the things we do and having friends like I do. Lord, thank You for giving me these blessings.

I nearly forgot about my journal tonight. We went on the Corvette factory tour. Now it's official, I'VE HAD ENOUGH CORVETTES!!!!!!!!! And it's true! It was 1-loud, 2-stinky, 3-tiring, 4-the tour guide wasn't very good (it was her first tour).

The restaurant we went to was great! It was right next to a river and you could see it through the leaves; it was beautiful! And the people were so friendly and nice.

Then we went to the museum of the Shakers, a religious group of people that think that Jesus already came back! They were called the Shakers because when they lived in Europe, before they immigrated here, the church would ridicule them because when they worshiped God they would shake their bodies. And they tried to have heaven on Earth. Like, there's no marriage in heaven so they didn't get married. And all the Shakers lived together and they had the house split in half so only the girls lived on the one side of the house and the guys lived on the other. And after meals they flipped their chairs upside down and hung them on the wall. It was interesting. There are only four Shakers left. Because there's no marriage, you have to convert to be a Shaker, you can't be born into it. We leave tomorrow to go home. I had a wonderful vacation!

We were walking by the park tonight and Morgan saw two large mushrooms here in Kentucky and she said, "This is mushroom country!"

November 14, 2008

Oh Lord, You have blessed me with the most wonderful of luxuries and the best of family You could have given me. Thank You for keeping us safe on our flight today, and getting us home to our Colorado. And You've given us a warm, well... cold welcome in giving us the snow. Thank You, for it ALL, God! For You are SOOO good! Amen.

Tonight I was reading "His Little Princess" to the girls and after, Claire started praying, "Dear God, please keep everyone okay, at least, everyone I know. And help me to be more like You. And thank You for letting me be Your princess."

November 16, 2008

We had church today. And potluck.

Noah and I made nine clues for Nate to solve. We are pretending we're major secret agents, trying to capture the Yugdab gang (it's bad guy backwards). It's a really fun game.

Dad and I went to the book store today during AWANA and American Girl had several new books. I got "Food and You".

Lord, I pray for Rebecca from church tonight. Help her overcome this illness. In Jesus' name, Amen.

November 17, 2008

I've had a fun night! Just last night I was telling

Dad, "I wish I could cook more." And Mom was rushing to get out the door for Tae Kwon Do (and they were going to stop at the library to get the next Little Britches book!) and told me to make dinner! From scratch! That was fun! And I told Mom this morning that I wished I had a writing desk (the kitchen is so unromantic) and Mom had to take the tea out of the schoolroom (Claire had another spill) so my little table was free... I moved it into the closet behind the door and have this journal and stationery on it! It's so nice!

Sophie (my friend from church that moved away) called me this afternoon and said, "I have some BIG news. Guess what it is."

After some guessing she said, "We're expecting." "What?" I didn't get it. "My mom's pregnant!"

When I told my mom she screamed! No really, she screamed! I'm SO happy for Sophie! Now she's the oldest of 6! I kind of am, too. Because of Mama's miscarriage with the twins, I'm kind of the oldest of 6 too. Actually we didn't even know she was pregnant (we as in, us kids).

I want to ask if the Reinharts can play tomorrow.

This afternoon Morgan tried to juice the clementines we got last night (she didn't succeed) and mashed M&M's and added them to the clementines. It wasn't very yummy. The pudding I made from scratch this afternoon was yummier. Tomorrow is a school day.

November 22, 2008

We took the wood chipper to the property and chipped a TON of wood and twigs and branches. And it was COLD! I wasn't doing much and read almost half of the 2nd Millie Keith book! I've had four bloody noses today. Ugh. We have church tomorrow and we're going to the Basset's for lunch. They're a fun family.

November 24, 2008

What an interesting day. Noah and I were in the schoolroom at 8am and didn't get started until 9am. I need help Lord, my attitude is getting the better of me; my anger too. I want to be YOUR girl and I need Your help. Amen.

November 25, 2008

What a day! First, we went to the Drummund's (a family from the homeschool group). Mrs. Drummund is helping get my dance skirt for the recital made and fitted. So now I don't have to borrow someone else's skirt. We had SO much fun with their kids. Then we went shopping. Then came home. It's 10:30pm, I need to get to bed and I still need to shower and everything. We also put the Christmas tree up today and put candy canes and colored lights on it. And it's BEFORE Thanksgiving! Isn't that funny?!? Noah and I did the counting for the candy contest for Thanksgiving today! The numbers are... I don't remember. Anyway, for the contest, you're supposed to guess how many pieces of candy are in the jar and the closest guess takes the jar home. Dad's five day weekend started tonight!

In this journal there is a section for trials. My trials are my attitude and my anger. I get mad at really dumb things! I need help from the Someone who can help with anything. Please help me overcome my anger.

Jesus, Rob had a minor heart attack and I praise You for keeping him safe. And I also pray for the safety, salvation, and needs of my Operation Christmas Child. Whoever she is. I pray the same for my relatives. And for Hannah Reinhart, because she is sick. Now I pray for myself. You know I have attitude problems and I need Your wonderful, conquering power and love to overcome this. In Jesus' name, Amen.

November 26, 2008

Another busy day! Dad went to the property until noonish and we decorated the tree. It's bedtime now so I need to hurry. People are coming at 1pm for the meal and I am determined to have a marvelous time no matter how crowded or noisy. I want to know how the contest for the candy jar goes. I want to know who wins.

I finished the 2nd Millie Book today and started "Laylie's Daring Quest" book. It's really good so far.

November 29, 2008

It snowed! It snowed almost 6" last night and Dad's taking us sledding out at the property!

P.M. We had a BLAST at the property. Dad pulled us on the sleds behind the Kubota. When Noah and I were riding, the sled handles broke and the second sled rope broke and whipped me across the leg. It hurt! Before that I fell off and landed on a cactus but only one little tine was poking me. After that we sledded down the back of the dam and had so much fun! After we got home I was doing dishes and leaned on that leg that I fell on and Mom dug four more cactus tines out of my leg. The Scotts came over and I had a lot of fun playing with the little kids.

December 1, 2008

I didn't write last night because we got home too late. We went to Mrs. Blake's surprise birthday party. We had a very fun, LATE night. The boys and I watched a movie.

This morning we made an igloo out of the snow left on the ground. Noah is a genius! He thought of making snow blocks out of Tupperware. Brilliant! We made a wall about two, maybe two and a half feet tall! Then we left for piano and I found out that my piano recital is THIS SATURDAY. Then, we took Noah and Morgan to Tae Kwon Do. Then Mama took Claire and me to the Littleton dance recital! It was beautiful. My God is SOOO good and strong and loving, sending His only Son to suffer for me!

We also went to the library and I got the 3rd Violet Book and put the 3rd Millie Book on hold. Morgan and Claire got their first library cards today! They are excited.

December 3, 2008

We got through a lot of choreography of our dance today. I got Mama's Christmas gifts at the Reinhart's church bookshop, "Names of Jesus" and "Fruit of the Spirit" pamphlets. I've decided to do a little study of my own on the Fruit of the Spirit. I'd like to start soon.

December 6, 2008

The piano recital went well. The Reinharts weren't able to come :(. They take lessons from Mrs. French too. Mrs. French had another teacher there and shared the recital with her.

We went to the bookstore after lunch (at Olive Garden) and I got a fairy book. We're going to the Malley's (church friends) for dinner tomorrow. I don't know what I'm gonna bring to keep me busy. I'll find something.

This section of the journal is for memories. I want to remember the time I was baptized. It was in Castle Rock in a neighborhood pool. All but Dad and Claire were baptized. The pool was green. Not normal. It just happened to have an algae problem.

The water I got baptized in! It was a happy day though.

Claire said, "I don't want to be baptized yet because I can't reach the bottom of the pool."

December 26, 2008

This section is to write as if I am talking to a friend. Which I am. God always hears me, and He cares. So I'll just write anything that pops into my head.

1 Thessalonians 5:16 "Be joyful always."

Lord, I want to pray for my Dad. Pray for his comfort. Whether he decides that we need to keep our dog Allie or not. I pray that we do what's best.

December 27, 2008

We had some friends over for dinner and while they were here Mama told me what her friend had just told her. "Mary was just saying how well you take care of your responsibilities."

Mary said, "It reminds me of one of my girls. I would need to tell her often 'I'm the mom. Me, not you.' Because she was so responsible she would forget who was in charge."

Mom looked at me and said, "Sound familiar?"

I am so happy and so proud to have been told (or someone noticed) that I take my responsibilities so well. I just pray that I can keep it up with a happy heart, a joyful spirit, a respectful tongue, and a kind, gentle, patient attitude.

3

1:00 AM 1-1-09

What an amazing last year! Look at all the things God has given me. I got my second degree black belt. My family bought 165 acres. I started other things too.

One thing is, God has shown me the Life of Faith books. The characters are like my friends, and inspire me to memorize Scripture. And taught me things I never really thought about. They have given me some good examples.

I think about what I have done this past year and wonder, what does God have in store for me this year?

Psalm 136:23 "Give thanks to the One who remembers us when things are going badly for us. His faithful love endures forever."

I want to remember this so I can remind myself and other people that His faithful love truly does endure forever.

1-4-09

Galations 5:15-18 "The Fruit of the Spirit is love, joy, peace, patience, kindness, faithfulness, gentleness, and self control. Against such things there is no law."

1 Timothy 4:12 "Let no one look down on you because you are young, but rather be an example for the believers in speech, conduct, love, faith and purity."

1 Thessalonians 5:15-18 "See that no one pays back another evil with evil, but always seek after that which is good for one another and for all people. Be joyful always. Pray continually; and in everything give thanks. For this is God's will for you in Christ Jesus."

Philippians 2:14 "Do not argue or complain."

Isaiah 43:1 "Thus says the Lord, your Creator, and He who formed you; 'Do not fear for I have redeemed you. I have called you by name, you are Mine.'"

I want to live by these verses.

1-5-09

Matthew 12:33 "Either make the tree good and its fruit good; or make the tree bad and its fruit bad;

for a tree is known by its fruit."

If we are the branches and God is the vine, what does this verse mean for me?

If God is the vine, then I grow out of Him. Anything that nourishes the vine flows through to nourish the branches. When a vine is sick, the branches die. Even if a branch is cut off of the vine, or the trunk, it will not kill the vine but it will still live or even grow a new branch. I am a branch. I am alive because of the vine. If there was no vine, I would die. This is a good pondering verse. I like to think about it.

1-6-09

There was a car accident on the road in front of our neighborhood last night. I want to thank You, Lord, for being with the person in the accident. For keeping him safe. Continue to be with him now and help him with whatever he needs. I also want to pray for his salvation. Thank You if he is already saved and if not, You can help this accident turn him towards You.

A few new things happened yesterday. I'm not supposed to tell anybody yet but I think it's okay. We're getting a puppy! She was born January 1st. Now shhh! Don't tell anyone!

1-18-09

This is my last week of being thirteen years old. I feel in this past year that I have grown closer to the Lord. There are some things I would like to do this year, goals really.

1) Grow even closer to Jesus.

2) Spread His wonderful word by my writing.

3) Love and care for those around me better, through His wisdom and guidance and love.

4) Be more like Him.

I can't think of any more right now but I'll try to write it down if I can think of some.

1-21-09

I praise You for giving me the best home and family I could ask for. Thank You for giving me a peaceful heart right now, help me to continue to have this wonderful feeling. I feel too grateful to express in words, but You know what is in my heart. Thank You, Jesus.

1-24-09

Yes, it is my 14th birthday! We haven't had dinner yet but I wanted to tell you about my party while it's still fresh in my memory.

First, I got up half an hour before people were supposed to be here!

The party was shopping in Elizabeth with Caroline and Hannah and Kirren. After they got here we did each others' hair for an hour, then left.

In Elizabeth, we went to a bookstore. I bought 'The Indian in the Cupboard' series. I got them for Noah for his birthday.

After that we had lunch at Sonic. Then, while we were eating I looked up and saw a truck pull up next to us and I thought, "That looks like Dad's truck." After two seconds, "Oh, look! Look it's Dad!" It was. That was really funny!

Then we went to Mainstreet in Elizabeth. We just walked Mainstreet and went in all the little shops and the library. We went to Chicadees and My Girlfriend's Closet. Then we went to Jabberwocky.

Then we went to the Carriage House. We all got Mom a bouquet of paper flowers that look like dried roses. And we all signed a card for her from my new stationery set to say thank you for taking us shopping.

At home we had some strawberry dessert and vanilla Italian soda. Kirren gave me a ONE WAY ticket to Mars to pick up the purple dog she got me. That's an on-going joke we have. I have a purple dog on Mars, so she made me this ticket. I had THE MOST fun I've had in a long time! Tonight I got hair stuff from my siblings. Oh, I forgot! Before we left this morning Mama gave me an envelope with a lovely card from everybody and money for shopping! I had an incredibly fun, memorable, exciting birthday!

Thank You, Lord, for giving me this day. Help me be a good example for my siblings and friends. Help me be the best fourteen year old I can be! I love You with all my heart.

3-30-09

I got a book from the library called, 'Discipline, the Glad Surrender' by Elizabeth Elliot. This is the book we're going through at dance. In it was a poem,

> 'Said the robin to the sparrow,
> 'I should really like to know
> why these anxious human beings
> rush about and worry so.'
> Said the sparrow to the robin,
> 'Friend, I think that it must be
> that they have no heavenly Father
> such as cares for you and me.'"

It's so true, we do rush around and worry like crazy. But like what 1 Peter 5:7 says, "Give all your worries to Him because He loves you."

4-14-09

In the Discipline book Elizabeth Elliot says, "When you have carried out your orders, you should say, 'We are servants and deserve no credit, we have only done our duty.'" This really stood out to me and I thought I should write it down.

Psalm 73:35 "I don't have anyone in heaven but You. I don't want anything on earth besides You."

Psalm 93 "The Lord rules. He puts on majesty as if it were clothes. The Lord puts on majesty and strength. The world is firmly set in place, it can't be moved. Lord, You began to rule a long time ago. You have always existed. Lord, the seas have lifted up their voice, they lifted up their pounding waves, but Lord, You are more powerful than the roar of the ocean, You are stronger than the waves of the sea. You are powerful in heaven. Your laws do not change, Lord. Your temple will be holy for all time to come."

4-16-09

Also, in this Discipline book there was a statement, "We are designed for good deeds."

I wanted to write it down as a reminder that, it's all not about you! The Lord created us for service to Him, not for ourselves.

4-24-09

I heard something and thought I'd like to remember it. It went sort of like this,

"Lord, I give You my mind. Sort through it, take away and get rid of all the bad and unnecessary stuff and leave the good things for me to ponder, remember, use, and to praise You with. Amen."

Oh Jesus, we've had an abundance of things happen in the last few days. I want to tell someone ALL about it.

First, we finished our dance! I am very excited!

Second, Dad broke his all time record of patients in one day! He got home late but saw so many people!

Third, we went to the bookstore and Morgan got the coolest pop-out pirate book ever! I bought Magic Tree House Book #41, AND 'Before Green Gables'!

Fourth, we went to the property today and there was 10' of water in the front pond! And the big pond towards the back was huge! HUGE! Katie (the dog) loves the water. It's so much fun to watch her play in it. Mom said we might be able to wade in it tomorrow. A man my parents hired is working on leveling out the 'driveway', or what will be the driveway someday. And he's digging the ponds deeper. That explains the 10' of water.

Fifth, Dad said to go to bed when I wanted to color a rose picture on a Bible Study page and I didn't feel any defiance! Thank You, Jesus!

Sixth, I felt all upset today 'cause of something I heard Mom say (don't want to say it) and I was feeling all horrible about myself so I opened my Bible and in all the random verses I read told me 'peace' and 'be patient'. I felt SO much better after that.

Seventh, Mom's been feeling kind of sick the past few days. I think she's gonna be fine, she was working hard at the property all day today then came home to company for dinner.

Eighth, AWANA Awards Night is in two days and I want to curl my hair.

Thank You for always listening, even when I'm rambling. Love You! Amen.

9-14-09

Father,

Blessed is everyone who fears the Lord, who walks in His ways. When you shall eat of the fruit of your hands, you will be happy and it will be well with you. Your wife shall be like a fruitful vine within your house, your children shall be like olive plants around your table. Behold, for thus shall the man be blessed who fears the Lord. The Lord bless you from Zion, and may you see the prosperity of Jerusalem all the days of your life. Indeed, may you see your children's children. Peace be upon Israel!

Psalm 128

Amen. I love You, Lord! XO

4

Well it is now 2010, Father, and I want to thank You for this new year.

Last year I:

- Went ice skating for the first time.
- I submitted a story in Patrick Henry College's short story competition (I didn't win but I entered it).
- I saw 'Seven Brides for Seven Brothers' (my new favorite movie!) this summer.
- I babysat the Stevens' for the Colorado homeschool conference.
- Our Kitchen flooded.
- I feel closer to my siblings and love them

more, though I still want to grow even closer to my siblings.
- This was my first year of high school!
- I got my first housekeeping job.
- And this past year was my first year to volunteer at Samaritan's Purse's Operation Christmas Child warehouse.

Psalm 139 "Search me, O God, and know my heart; Try me and know my anxious thoughts; and see if there be any hurtful way in me, and lead me in the everlasting way."

Psalm 119:34-35 "Give me understanding, that I may observe Your law and keep it with all my heart. Make me walk in the path of Your commandments, for I delight in it."

I love You, Lord. Help me to be who You want me to be. In Jesus' name, Amen.

P ray everyday

R etreat to a quiet place

A sk Him everything

Y ou are His child so He will listen to all you say

E rase all unholy thoughts

R emember He cares about all of your cares

MY 2010 GOALS
1. Grow closer and know Him more.
2. Love my family more and treat them as they treat me.
3. Be influenced by God and godly people, not

        by the world.
4.   Cook more and learn more about it.
5.   Improve my dancing skills.

2-12-10
Father,
Claire has a horrible cough and stuffy nose.
Please heal her. Oh Great Physician, please, make
her better soon.
        Psalm 41:3
        "The Lord nurses them when they are sick and
eases their pain and discomfort."
        I trust You, my King, You know what's best. You
have a plan. I love You. In Jesus' name, Amen.
        2-14-10
        2 Peter 1:5-8, 10-11 "Now for this very reason
also, applying all diligence, in your faith supply
moral excellence, and in your moral excellence,
knowledge, and to your knowledge, self-control, and
in your self-control perseverance, and in your perseverance, godliness, and in your godliness, brotherly
kindness and in your brotherly kindness, love. For
if these qualities are yours and are increasing they
render you neither useless nor unfruitful in the true
knowledge of our Lord Jesus Christ. For as long as
you practice these things, you will never stumble; for
in this way the entrance into the eternal kingdom of
our Lord and Savior Jesus Christ will be abundantly
supplied to you."

3-2-10

Father in Heaven,

I have had a hard time these past few days not getting angry toward my siblings and controlling my frustration when being set off by the simplest things. I don't understand. There are so many verses that say, 'self-control, self-control'. Maybe You're showing me that I need to work on my self-control and now that I look back on the past few days I do need to watch my attitude. I found a verse I had highlighted, Ephesians 4:31, 'Let all bitterness and wrath and anger and clamor and slander be put away from you.' Then I prayed and did better today. Really better. Thank You, Father. You are so loving! Thank You for helping me today and help me to continue getting better everyday. I love You so much.

4-10-10

Father,

It has been wonderful studying Ruth in Precepts. Thank You for being my Kinsman Redeemer.

Lord, I pray for my dad. He works so hard. Bless him. Send lots and lots of patients to his office. Since the health care bill has been in action, work has been much slower. We know You will always provide for us. Thank You for reassuring us of Your unlimited love.

I am a bit worried about school. I'm not doing well in math. Help me to catch up. Assist me in holding down the 'record' button in my brain and not lose the tape. I'm kind of having a hard time with that at dance too. And thank You for gifting me with a body that is physically able to dance.

Last week, I had a feeling, "What good am I?" I doubted that I was useful or good at anything. But You made me just the way I am. Help me learn how I could be more helpful. You are so amazing and wonderful! I love You!

4-17-10

My prayer today, Lord, is this:

"Search me, O God, and know my heart; Try me and know my anxious thoughts; And see if there is any hurtful way in me, and help me in the everlasting way." Psalm 139:23-24

4-19-10

Oh Father,

A few months ago a Jehovah Witness came to our door. The man came back again today with a woman. They were here for about an hour and a half! They came wanting to discuss the Bible with Mama. So she got her Revelation and Genesis studies out along with her Bible and concordance. They argued for a long time never answering Mama's questions, but changing the subject or asking another question. Noah and I were out with her, too. I understood all Mama said and was very proud at the way she stood for You, and was sure that You were smiling at her. And, with Your help, she asked just the right questions she needed to ask the Jehovah Witnesses. You were there, Lord. Thank You! Mama asked the lady if she believed she was going to heaven. She said she believed she wouldn't. I am full of sympathy for her. She believes that she will be on earth or helping You reign (that part wasn't quite clear).

Anyway, at the end of the hour and a half Mama got the concordance out and they started another argument and after the guy said something like, "The Bible is the most important book. I'm not gonna trust something some man wrote, the Bible is more important!" Mama had NOT been implying that the concordance was more important than the Bible. Mama looked at me with a they-just-won't-admit-I'm-right-look and said, "Am I being clear, Maddie?"

I said, "I understand you." And the guy went on about some man writing a concordance 'being the Bible' or something that Mama hadn't said. I couldn't hold it in anymore! Especially after I had already spoken. I said, "She did NOT say that! I went on about what a concordance is, what it does and helps with, and that it is NOT the Bible! When I was done explaining, the lady said, "What she means is it's a tool to understand the meanings of words in the original language."

It felt great backing up Mama, standing up for my beliefs, and defending Your word. The guy said, "Oh, I just misunderstood." Afterwards Mama said I was awesome. When they were leaving both said I did well at explaining and he asked, "How old are you?"

"I am 15." I had a tone in my voice, I could tell.

"Wow, you carry yourself like you were 19 or 21."

He had said 'next time' so we know he's coming back. We're gonna be ready though. Thank You for being with us today, and helping us say the right things.

Psalm 25:4-5 "Make me know Your ways, O Lord, teach me Your paths. Lead me in Your truth and teach me. For You are the God of my salvation, for You I wait all the day."

4-21-10

"How great Thou art! Then sings my soul!" I love You so much!

We finished our dance today (our song is 'Mistaken' by Aaron Shust). I'm really excited! I am constantly amazed at how You have Your hand in everything.

With the Jehovah Witnesses, their false doctrine is mostly in Genesis and Revelation! That's what Mama has been studying for the past four years! I wonder what Your plans are for me. How it's all going to work together just right.

5-2-10

Oh Father!

I've been wanting to write You so bad (okay, not that bad) for the past few days.

First, we only have four more days left in school! I'm almost done with my first year of high school!

We weren't sure how many more days left of school, so Mama checked yesterday and only four! Yay!

Second, we got cows! They're pretty, and they're super cool!

Next, I wanted to thank You for helping me with my patience yesterday. Morgan fell off her scooter and scraped her knee and wouldn't let me look at it, let alone clean it. Thanks for helping me bottle up most of my frustration (forgive me for being a little angry), and help me to continue getting better at it.

Next, I pray that You bring Grandma here safely and be with Grandpa while she's gone. I pray this week goes well. And be with Mama. Keep her stress free. She's so, so busy this week. And I pray for myself, Lord. For patience, kindness, gentleness, and self-control. And to get lots of school work done, and help our dance recital go well. In Jesus' name, Amen.

5-11-10

Oh Lord! My dance recital went wonderfully last night. I marvel at Your immeasurable love, Father. I love praising You through dance. Thank You for a company like Celebration Ministry of Arts.

Psalm 2 talks about how You will always be with me even though I don't deserve You, and how You protect those who take refuge in You. Psalm 3:3 says, "But You, O Lord, are a shield about me, my glory, and the One who lifts my head."

There isn't even a word to describe how wonderful, loving, just, and caring You are. You were greatly praised last night, Father. During rehearsal, I saw how powerful the songs were! I almost cried. I am SO happy this session is one I got the video for. I love You, Father!

5-17-10

For Hannah's birthday I gave her a verse. Thank You SO much for wonderful Christian sisters like her! Thank you, Father!

Hosea 2:1 "Call your brothers, 'my people' and call your sisters, 'my loved one.'"

6-14-10

Oh Father,

We just finished studying Ruth and Kinsman Redeemer. It overwhelms me, Lord, to think You, the Most High God, want to redeem me, a sinner. "Redeem" means so much to me now.

Just learning about what a redeemer does overwhelms me. The promises You have given to redeem us are amazing. I learned that the requirements for a redeemer are to: protect and preserve the family name, and/or their property by buying back the family land that was sold to pay a debt. Protecting and preserving the relatives life by buying back the relative who sold themselves into slavery to pay a debt. Or by being a blood avenger. It's so amazing! And the redeemer must be a close relative! I love You Lord! Isaiah 43:1 "Fear not for I have redeemed you, I have called you by name, you are Mine."

I want to thank You for all of the job opportunities I have received already this summer. Please help me not to be prideful about my work, but to be humble.

And Father, I would like to thank You for the blessing of rain we've had these past four days. We needed it. Oh! And thank You for helping us find our camper. It's really cool!

6-15-10

Psalm 116 I LOVE this chapter! Oh God, You are so great!

7-16-10

Oh Lord,

I pray for Grandma and Grandpa Otto while they get ready for us to visit. Grandpa doesn't feel well most of the time, so help him, Father. And please be with Grandma while she cares for him.

Father, I pray for the president. I know You are in control. Lord, but be with him anyway.

Oh! And I got an iPod! I don't understand this feeling though. I don't know why (the real reason) I got it. Perhaps it was the thought of sharing it with my family. I don't think I bought it just because I thought it would be cool and I had the money. I don't want to be selfish. But I'm pretty excited! And I'm glad I got it before our Kansas trip!

I love You. In Jesus' name, Amen.

Oh! And Father, please help me be a woman after

Your own heart and do what is right in Your eyes.

8-4-10

Oh Father,

I pray that You will be with the neighbor family. Babysitting them this summer was difficult for me. The kids aren't very kind to each other. I know You put me there for a reason but I am glad I'm done with them this summer. They were rude and disrespectful and worst of all they don't know You (the way my family does). I tried to be patient but it saddens me, Father, to see how they treat each other. I pray You can use the time I had with them to have an impact on the kids. Thank You for giving me a family who fears You. I love You. Be with their family. In Your Son's name, Amen.

11-15-10

Lord,

So much has happened since I wrote last. I think the biggest thing is, we found out Mama R. has breast cancer. Be with her Father. I lift her into Your loving, healing hands.

I have started babysitting for the Bakers on Tuesdays for 2 hours.

Grandpa Terry came to visit. We went hiking and swimming and biking. It finally snowed! While we were swimming of all times! So, of course, we went to get ice cream. What better thing to do during the first snow than go swimming and eat ice cream? It's tradition!

My family has been on vacation already. We went to Branson, Missouri, and saw Cirque montage (former artists of Cirque du soleil). I really enjoyed that. We went to Silver Dollar City, which was super fun! We played mini golf, went to the Dixie Stampede (really cool), visited the Browns (my cousin Rachel took me out to a coffee shop) and we visited Grandma and Grandpa Otto. We also saw the Passion Play in Eureka Springs, Arkansas. And that day we stopped at an Amish store and wound up ordering a hope chest for my 16th birthday! It was such a fun vacation.

This past weekend Mama and I went on our first women's retreat together. It was SO fun!

I get my wisdom teeth out this next week. Lord, give me strength and courage. I know it'll be fine but I am still a little nervous.

Oh! I forgot! Noah and I started a geometry class with Mrs. Silven and I am really enjoying it. And I started worldview class with Mrs. Brachen and I am really enjoying that too. And I am studying Exodus with Mrs. Lewis and am loving that too!

Thank You for all that You have done.

11-19-10

Father,

Yesterday I got my wisdom teeth pulled. It was rough but thank You that today was much better. This day has gone way, way faster than yesterday.

Help me heal quickly, Jehovah Rapha, You are so wonderful.

A few days ago we learned that Mama R. has stage 2 cancer and it is not as bad as we thought it could be. Thank You, Jehovah Rapha!

11-27-10

Lord Jesus,

We have so much to be thankful for.

I started reading through Ezekiel. It's very interesting and exciting. I wonder what the spirit was, or symbolized. And I have been reading about David's life. I guess it never really registered in my head that the same David who killed Goliath, had problems with Saul, and who fathered Solomon was all the same guy.

I ask that You can help me to continue getting along with my 'neighbors', those You've placed around me. And Jehovah Shalom, Lord of peace, help me remain calm and keep a peaceful spirit when I see the holes in my mouth from the wisdom teeth surgery. And please heal those holes quickly.

And be with the Reinhart family, heal Mama R's body. I love You Jehovah Raah, because You are my Shepherd.

11-29-10

Praise the Lord! I was going to write and pray that I won't get infection in my wisdom tooth holes and I pray I won't get dry sockets. So, I didn't get a syringe from the doctor, so the holes in my mouth get food in it and I can't get it clean. Mama said she might have something we could use for a syringe and she came back upstairs with an eyedropper and a water balloon! We used it and now I feel clean! It's just another step in this adventure! Father, thank You!

Be with the Reinharts, and Mama R.

I love You Father, let Your will be done and we'll give You the praise. Amen.

12-16-10

"For everything there is a season. A time for sorrow and a time for rejoicing." Ecclesiastes 3:1-8

Jehovah Shalom (Lord is peace),

Please give peace. To the Reinharts and the Reeds.

Oh Father, Mr. Reeds has died. We don't wholly understand but we trust You. Be with their daughter and her precious heart. Keep it pure and help her grow toward You in this hard time. Protect their other daughter and son's hearts too, they are all hurting. And Mrs. Reeds. She must be confused and hurt and sad. Be with them and those who are close to them, like my Mama and Daddy. We are all hurting.

Yet there is a time to rejoice too! Mama R's surgery went perfectly well! The surgeon finished 3 hours early. She went home today. Mama O. (my mama) saw her and said that even though Mama R. was on drugs she was fine! Just sore but she could move her arms. Thank You Jesus! We give You the praise! Please continue to heal her and give peace to her and her family. In Your wonderful, wonderful name! Amen.

12-25-10
Happy Birthday Jesus! I love You!

12-26-10
Jesus,

I had such a wonderful Christmas! Thank You for putting me in such a home!

I've been thinking, am I selfish? If You asked me to go to Africa or somewhere else, would I do it? I have no desire to go anywhere. I want to be a light, but here in Colorado.

I talked to Mama and Dad, and they said one way You lead us is by giving us a desire. And we need lights here. Although I think that I have a fear of sadness, I have a very sheltered home with loving, godly parents. You have blessed me more than I know. Thank You Jesus!

"The darker the sky, the brighter the stars shine."

12-31-10
The last day of 2010. So much has happened this year.

- I got my first iPod.
- This was my first year going to the Civil War Ball.
- Noah and I started geometry and I started

Worldview.

- I got a hope chest even though it's for my 16th birthday.
- Mama R was diagnosed with breast cancer and is now recovering. I have realized the seriousness and reality of cancer.
- Mr. Reeds is no longer with us.
- Our Thanksgiving party had no more than 30 people! That's a small crowd!

As for last year's goals:

1. Grow closer to Him. I feel that I have. Especially after studying Ruth.

2. Love my family more and treat them as they treat me. Yes, but it could always use a little more work.

3. Be influenced by God and godly people not by the world. Definitely yes.

4. Cook more. Yeah, some.

5. Improve my dancing skills. Yes, I think I have a little. It could use some more work.

MY 2011 GOALS:

1. I want to be a godly influence to those around me and I want to shine for Jesus
2. I want to be a worthy, godly, gentle, kind, respectful, willing… sister, daughter and friend
3. I want to be a responsible driver
4. I would like to be able to do the front splits

by the end of this year

5. I want to read through the Bible this year
   and memorize more Scripture

5

Father, Sometimes I worry about myself. You hold my heart but sometimes I find myself thinking about some gentlemen friends a little more than I, I don't know, more than I like. You know what I mean. I find myself thinking about a certain one, then switch to someone else. I don't like the feeling. I am closer (and absolutely will continue being closer) to my girlfriends. It's okay to have guy friends.

Probably when I read this later it won't make much sense but writing helps me sort out the things boggling around in my mind and my heart. Please take this awkward feeling away. Thank You for always listening to me and helping me (I already feel better). You probably felt awkward when You were my age too sometimes.

1-31-11

James 4:8 "Draw close to the Father and He will draw close to you."

1 Corinthians 3:23 "You belong to Christ and Christ belongs to God."

Jehovah Rapha,

I have uttered that name so often lately and heard it spoken by others yet it is still as reassuring and comforting as it ever was. Lord, Mama doesn't 'do sick' very well. And she gets horrendous sinus issues when she gets a cold. Father, heal her. Ease her discomfort. Help no one else get this. In Jehovah Rapha's holy name, Amen.

3-2-11

Lord Jesus,

Touch my angry, defiant heart. Tame my pride. Please give me humility sufficient enough to overcome this trial.

Father, I've started driving. And tension has risen between Mama and I when I drive (and other times lately). My heart becomes angry and defiant. Forgive me and help me overcome my pride, which I think is behind this storm. I need to humble myself but my pride is strong, I need You to help me conquer and I will give You the praise. Thank You Jesus.

Lord,

I have felt rather crummy about myself lately. I just have to write this and get these feelings out of my system. Father, I love the family You gave me so much. I need You to help me overcome this 'me' and 'my way' selfishness stuff. But inside, it feels like a rebellious teenager wants to come out! It saddens me to know I have hurt someone I love by being disrespectful, rude, immature, or by losing my temper. They deserve a better attitude. You, Yourself said all things are possible in You, God, and You are greater than anything and we can conquer through You! Hallelujah!

I don't know if it's my schedule that's stressing me out and drives my immaturity and anger, but whatever it is Lord, forgive me. I have sinned against Your commandment by not honoring my parents. I am sorry. You see my heart and know how sad and repentant it is. Give me the self control to hold my tongue. Give me strength to keep my temper in check.

Oh, thank You Father! You are so wonderful and forgiving, thank You for Your mercy. I feel so, so much better with that out of me. Ahh. I bless You and praise You. Amen.

Haggai 1:7 "Thus says the Lord, consider your ways!"

Isaiah 26:20 "Come my people, enter into your

rooms and close the doors behind you; hide for a little while until indignation runs its course."

Psalm 3:3 "But You, O Lord, are a shield about me, my glory, and the One who lifts my head."

Romans 8:37 "But in all these things we over-whelmingly conquer through Him who loves us."

6-27-11

Oh Jesus,

We have had such a crazy last week. But before I write it down I want to praise You for Your faithfulness. For bringing Mama R through her chemo and reconstruction. And for the speed at which the hospital responded to Benjamin Blake's broken arm.

Last Thursday, it was the first day of the home-school conference and I was babysitting the Stevens'. We rearranged the girls bedrooms and played with my parachute and had a lot of fun. Small group was last night. I have to say, Noah and Millie (age 3) are so cute! We were watching 'Goofy' and Millie crawled up into the crook of Noah's arm which he had slung over the back of the couch, and she stayed there all night, tee hee. I can just see someone asking Noah if he has a girlfriend and him saying, 'Yep she's blonde with pigtails, about 2'8" and around 30 lbs.' So cute! Anyway…

Friday was Mama R's surgery and all the Reinhart kids came here. We had a great time.

Sunday was Father's Day. Thank You Father, for

giving me such an awesome Daddy down here. I love him so much. That night we went to Tim Hawkin's comedy show.

Morgan's 10th birthday party was the next day. The party was fun, easy and kinda wet with all the water balloons.

Tuesday, Dad comes downstairs with news that Benjamin broke his arm and is having surgery. Wednesday, Mama and I picked up Nate and Lou and Rachel and took them to the hospital in Denver. Poor Ben. He was watching a movie and was kind of out of it. Well, Nate, Lou and Rachel spent the night. PARTY WEEK!

Thursday rolls around again, the Blake kids go home and we hang out. Friday and Saturday we're building fence in 90 degree weather, both days. Lord, Daddy hurt himself. Heal him quickly.

Sunday, Morgan is 10 years old! She is such a blessing, she always makes me laugh, she is like a drop of sunshine. We went to lunch after church and Dad took the other kids to see Cars 2 in theaters (I'm a little jealous). Mama and I went to a gradu-ation party at church for Diana and a couple other girls. You have blessed the world with those girls. Thank You for putting them in my life.

And that has been my week.

This morning we flew through a whole module of science. Test and all! And I got done with ALL of my chores and went on a walk AND I lifted weights today. Now I'm here soaking in the tub writing the 5th page of this novel of my last week. And praising You for Your faithfulness through the trials and loving You for the sweet times. I love You Jesus, Amen.

7-5-11

Lord,

I have found myself getting angry and frustrated with people, especially my dear and special family. So I pray, Father, You can help me overcome these emotions with the fruit of Your Spirit. Love, Joy, Peace, Patience, Kindness, Goodness, Faithfulness, Gentleness and Self Control as in Galatians 5:22. I have found myself calling Noah names and telling him to shut up just because I'm annoyed.

I talked to You about it last night and today. I look back at today and I didn't get frustrated almost at all. Thank You! I praise You! If I may add to the above about getting angry with my family, that I love them too much to intentionally hurt them. But the words aren't being stopped. Thank You for helping me.

7-12-11

Triumph! Father, thank You for helping me overcome my frustration I had been feeling toward my family. Please continue to help me triumph over this. Victory today but I still continue the fight against myself. Father, I have another trial. I really try not to but I think I've been a little judgmental lately. Please forgive me. I'm not trying to be, I'm trying not to!

Isn't judging looking down on or maybe changing an opinion of someone? After something happens maybe? Help me Lord! Help me conquer this trial! In Your Holy Name, Amen.

8-3-11

Father,

There is a girl in one of my classes who's dad has cancer and is not doing well.

I can't stop bad and awful things from happening but through these things happening around us we can find comfort and strength in You. I can't stop these but You can. Again, You are in control. You make good things happen for and through those who love You. Thank You.

Marta returns to Spain today. Give her a safe flight and help her to not feel so restless.

Father, be with the people who survived the tsunami a few years ago. Send missionaries to Thailand to teach the people there that there is no pain where You are.

And Haiti's people (earthquake), and Japan's people (earthquakes), and the people of North Africa which I have just heard are at war. Show them where eternal peace is found. Be with the people in Missouri as well. It is hard to know that there is devastation in the country where I live. And the world that I live in. Thank You for keeping us all safe and healthy. I can't handle knowing a lot of these things but You can help me bear it.

8-8-11

1 Thessalonians 5:17 "Pray continually."

El Olam, I praise You for bringing our family home safely from Kansas. We had a nice time. It was nice to see everybody, and my cousin Luke before he goes back to Cambodia. And Claire and I danced at Grandma's church. I want to honor You and bless others too through dance, and it was cool to have that opportunity.

Sleeping in Kansas made me nervous though after I found a cricket in my hair one night and heard the 'tarantula-in-the-house-3-days-after-we-left-last-time' story. That actually is the whole story.

But while we were there Mama told me that I have a sarcasm issue and I flare up over unnecessary things.

Thank You for helping me through my judgmental and pride problems. I ask You now, to please help me be like Jesus. To talk and think the way He would. And think of others before myself. Sometimes I feel like I complain and whine all about me and worry about me-me-me. This needs to be changed.

I love You Lord and I trust You. In Your Son's name, Jesus my Savior, let it be so.

8-15-11

God, what is wrong with me!? Why have I been so horrible to everyone lately? I don't understand!

Why can't things make sense in math and science? Why can't I be easier to get along with? Is it pride? Mom said I've been this way for about a month! I'm crying out to You! Help me! Fix my heart. Show me what to do differently. I don't want my family to dread being around me. Please show me what's causing this. I need You!

8-28-11

Father,

Thank You for helping me through what was going on above. I think it was a couple things. I was PMS-ing early and all the next week. I'm not making excuses, I think it probably was a heart problem as well. Lord, I want to continue giving You my thoughts, conversations and actions. I trust that You will make pleasant things come out of my mouth. I pray for this next school week. Please help me learn, and understand easily with no dramatic scenes like last week.

Father, I started a new book called 'In His Steps' by Charles Sheldon. It's about, 'What does following Jesus mean?' The characters decide to go a whole year and not do anything before asking What Would Jesus Do? This is a strong, powerful thing and very honoring. And the results were amazing. I want to start doing that very thing. Ask 'What would You do?' in ordinary situations, in daily life. Will You help me? This will improve my character I think and most definitely help me shine brighter for You.

In Yeshua's beautiful name, let it be so.
9-27-11

Three days ago Daddy surprised us by coming upstairs (after we were all ready for church) and announcing, "Change your clothes, we're going to the mountains today."

It was like a day of vacation. We listened to Pastor Ed (Calvary Chapel Aurora) on Grace FM on our way to Estes Park.

We went to Rocky Mountain National Park. We climbed up rocks next to a waterfall and went up past the tree line. I bought Morgan a rock key chain for Christmas. What a memorable day! Apparently we spent 5 hours in the park but it didn't feel like much time at all. Then we spent the rest of the day shopping. It was SOOO much fun! I would love to spend another day up there. Maybe even for my birthday!

I love Daddy; he is so thoughtful. Taking us up there, laughing, spending time with each other, shopping. And he bought us a pound of taffy (of which we only had 2 pieces left after dinner) and of course we got fudge. Daddy, so sweet, wanted to top the day off for us to make it the best day, so he finished it off by taking us to get pizza! It really was the best day!

And one of the coolest parts is. I had been feelin' lazy at school, thinking, "I need some sort of break." But I didn't tell anyone. And surprise! Dad takes us to the mountains! Thank You Jesus, just like in Matthew 5, 'The Father knows what you need even before you ask Him.' Praise God! And thank You for my Daddy.

10-20-11

Jesus,

Since I have written last Mr. Lansky is no longer with us. My heart breaks for their family. You are Jehovah-Jireh, the One who will always provide. They are hurting, Lord. Continue to help them.

Tonight, Dr. Given called to say they wouldn't make it to small group because Taylor Stafford is in the hospital. God, I am scared for her but the doctors say she will be okay. Please bring her safely out of the hospital tonight, comforted and trusting You still more. We all trust You, El Shaddai, the All Sufficient One. So true, You are completely sufficient. I love You. You say in Your word, 'Perfect love casts out all fear.' so I ask You to cast the fear out of their family right now.

And last week my Great Grandma Pat died. I don't know where she was in a relationship with You but Your plan never fails and You always, always know best. I trust You. I am so grateful Lord, thank You for keeping my family so safe and so healthy. You have blessed us greatly. Psalm 4:8, "In peace I lie down and sleep, for You alone, O LORD , make me to dwell in safety." Amen, Amen, Amen.

10-25-11

Lord Jesus,

I ask You to relieve my dad from his stresses, pains and worries. He has been so stressed out lately and last night he had a headache so bad he had to go lay down. And he has a cold. The office is pretty slow these days so I pray that lots of people come and insurance companies start doing their jobs and the President will realize what results some of his decisions have made.

I trust You, Lord. I know You will always provide, but I still ask You to relieve Dad who works so hard for us.

Father, there are so, so many sad, horrible, frightening things going on in the world lately. And I pray that You will keep us safe and healthy. And I pray for the Lanskys as they continue to heal. And Taylor also and the decisions her family needs to make, and the friends of the Stevens who just lost a daughter to a car accident. And I pray for healing for those hurting and frightened from all the disasters around the world.

And I thank You for saving me.

10-27-11

Jehovah Shammah (the Lord my Companion),

I feel frightened. I get this way when a lot of grief is around me or when something disastrous happens in the world or when I think about the holocaust and WWII. Such horrible things happened. I get this depressed, anxious mood, worried about what might happen.

'Perfect love casts out fear.'

'Don't worry, tomorrow will take care of itself.'

'I will never leave you or forsake you.'

These promises lift me up. They are so true.

Please, please, please keep my family safe and healthy. I trust You but it would be wonderful if You would always keep us perfectly, perfectly safe.

11-11-11

Yesterday after Bible study Mrs. Lewis told me that I was wise for my age and to always thank You for it. And I do, Father. Thank You so much, help me to use it for Your glory.

Mama started telling Mrs. Lewis about the compliments she has received about me. Mrs. Lewis said, "You shine so brightly. People see something in you that isn't in most other people. It's like, you are a princess in the midst of commoners, and they see you and think 'There is a princess among us, why is she here? What is this magnificence around her? What can I do to be like that?"

It was beautifully said and later, it made me cry. Thank You for Mrs. Lewis.

My prayer, Lord, is that You continue allowing me to be Your mirror and reflect Your light and love. Please let them look through me and see You.

12-28-11

Father, I heard a prayer of thanks that I wanted to remember because it is short but powerful.

"For food in a world where there is hunger,

For faith in a world where there is fear,

For friendship in a world where so many walk alone.

For this we give thanks. Amen"

6

1-1-12

So strange. A new year already. Well, last year I:

- Learned to drive and finished all of my day-time driving hours back in April
- I started Worldview II class
- Mama R is well and healthy and I feel closer to Hannah and Caroline
- My family are wintering cattle for the first time this year
- I have found a new love (passion, really) for socks. The busier and crazier and mismatched the better
- I've finally been to Operation Christmas Child more than once in a season, Yay!

- Daddy hired me as a ranch hand and I love it

How I did on lasts year's goals:

1. Shine for Jesus. In October we went to Disney for vacation and I was constantly praying that I'd shine. One night that week Mama was telling me goodnight and she said, "You shone so bright today. I feel like I see Jesus when I look at you." I almost cried.
2. Be a worthy sister/daughter/friend. I always try my hardest but don't always feel worthy.
3. Be a responsible driver. Mama says I am but I can't be over-confident.
4. Middle splits. Nope. I'm maybe 9" away, but nope.
5. Read through the Bible. Mostly. I'm in Philippians; I'm still working on it. So close! But no, I didn't finish in the past year.

MY 2012 GOALS:

1. Be a responsible and very careful driver in my first year of having my license
2. I'd like to start cosmetology school and maybe get another job
3. I want to be able to do the middle splits by the end of this year
4. Memorize apologetics verses (references and all) that are in my Worldview notes (both from WVI and WVII)

5. Be more flexible and 'go with the flow' when
    my plans change

Lord Almighty,

I pray over this coming year. I pray for this
coming presidential election that will happen later
this year and for the government and the economy.
Please ease Daddy's work stresses, please make them
lighter and easier to bear. Father, please remind us
every day about what You have done. I pray for good
health and protection over our family and over those
who are dear to us and to You. And I pray for our
church and the families and elders of our church. I
love and trust You, God. In Jesus' Name, Amen.

1-23-12

Father,

Today is my last day of being 16. Now I won't be
able to sing 'You are 16 going on 17' and call it my
song! That was my theme song for my whole 16th
year.

I was reading my Bible last night and a few verses
stood out to me. I want them to become a steady
part of my life. Please help them to take root in my
heart and grow tall and strong.

2 Timothy 2:22-25

"Now flee from youthful lusts and pursue righteousness, faith, love and peace with those who cry
out to the Lord from a pure heart. But refuse foolish
and ignorant speculations, knowing that they produce quarrels. The Lord's bondservant must not be

quarrelsome but be kind to all, able to teach, patient when wronged, with gentleness correcting those who are in opposition."

4-22-12

Sermon Notes:

1 Corinthians 3:5-17

"For we are God's fellow workers; you are God's field, God's building... each man's work will become evident; for the day will show it because it is to be revealed with fire, and the fire itself will test the quality of each man's work."

Today the gospel is 'all about me' and 'God is all love'. No, God is a God of wrath, justice and righteousness! People today (unbelievers and some believers even) have no concept of a wrathful God. For example: Heaven is a stadium and I'm fighting for a better seat than you but in the end we'll all get there and when we do we'll see that there are no seats! So, all that pushing and fighting was in vain.

Matthew 19:30 "But many who are first will be last, and the last, first."

5-8-12

Tonight the Dolens took Claire and me to the Castle Rock CMA dance recital. The theme this session was the 'Name of Jesus' and the power of His name. She talked about how we are ambassadors for Christ. I just loved one of the examples she gave.

Say a dad asked his little girl to go fetch brother

for dinner. She does but brother says, 'You can't tell me what to do.' But what if she said, 'Dad said to come down for dinner.' There is authority behind her words. It's the same way with God. We speak and He is the authority behind what we say.

Lord Jesus, Holy Spirit, use me. Let me be Your hands, and feet, and voice. Let others look at me and see You. In Jesus' name, Amen.

5-20-12

Lord,

Help me burn my burden. I want to burn it and give You the ashes. I don't want it anymore. In Jesus the Messiah's name, Amen.

5-27-12

Noah's 15 today!

Sermon Notes:

God has a missionary heart. So, He made the world a mission field. And He has a mission agency called The Church. He also only had one Son, He was a missionary. His program: Matthew 28:19 "Go and make disciples of all nations, baptizing them in the name of the Father, and the Son, and the Holy Spirit. Teaching them to observe all that I commanded you. And lo, I am with you always, even to the end of the age."

5-29-12

Jehovah the Comforter,

Thank You for Your mercy and Your perfect timing. I am not home, I am at my dear friends the

Reinharts house for the 'Set-Apart Girl Conference'.

My family has to put our little dog Meg to sleep tomorrow morning at 8am, and I cannot be there to comfort them. But again, maybe Your perfect timing and Your plan was for me not to be at home.

There couldn't be a more perfect time though, (our female Katie had a litter of puppies and my brother kept one of them) Hazel is 7 weeks old and will need a lot of attention. I thank You that Katie didn't get pregnant with Daubs before, like we wanted, because that wasn't Your plan and that would have been her first litter, not now when we need it.

Thank You for the 11 years we've had with Meg and the many, many memories we have of her. But I know my family is hurting badly. And I can't be there! My heart is hurting! I trust You will comfort them and heal us quickly.

I love You. I see just a part of Your plan, and it's perfect. Ecclesiastes 3:1 "There is an appointed time for everything, for every event under heaven."

Romans 8:28 "Everything works together for the good of those who love God."

God, I praise You and am on my knees thanking You a hundred times over that it's just the dog. It is not one of my sisters or my parents or my brother. Thank You! Thank You! Thank You!

6-3-12

Be the kind of woman that, in the morning when her feet hit the floor, the Devil says, 'Oh no! She's up!'

6-10-12

Psalm 45:9-17 "King's daughters are among Your noble ladies… Listen, O daughter, give attention and incline your ear: forget your people and your father's house; then the King will desire your beauty because He is your Lord, bow down to Him. The King's daughter is all glorious within; her clothing is interwoven with gold. She will be led to the King in embroidered work; They will be led forth with rejoicing and gladness. They will enter into the King's palace. Therefore the peoples will give You thanks forever and ever."

Hallelujah!

6-14-12

Father,

I praise You for Your faithfulness. You helped me get rid of my burden. Thank You for helping me burn the old Maddie. It has taken weeks, but I don't feel her anymore!

And You blessed me through Mama by her saying, "The things that usually frustrate you haven't been. Good job." But I know that last bit was for Your credit.

You have used Mama before. The first time, I remember, I had begged You to give me a humble heart. At the end of the week Mama was telling me good night and she told me that I had been humble during the week. I ran (literally) upstairs and locked myself in the bathroom and sobbed with my hands raised high for half an hour. And then, last year on vacation I asked You if people could look at me and see You. If I could just be a mirror with Your reflection. And again, at bedtime Mama told me, "You shone today, my dear." I hadn't even told her.

Yahweh, it seems I have been praying for so many people and places lately. You know, I think this world's birth pangs that you told us about in Revelation are becoming daily occurrences. It is painful.

I've been praying for cousin my Luke. I don't hear much about what he is doing in Cambodia but please guide him and give him wisdom in the decisions he is and will be making.

And then there is my dance teacher, Miss Miranda, who's going all over the globe on the World Race mission trip doing what must be done for the expansion of Your kingdom. Some of the places she will be going are dangerous but You promised 'I will NEVER leave you.' She is different than anyone I have ever met before. She is passionate, and strong, and gentle, and very graceful, and amazing, and just right for the task before her.

God, I just ache for Africa. Sudan, South Sudan, Democratic Republic of the Congo, and Uganda.

The terrorists are doing their work killing, enslaving, raping, kidnapping, bombing and hurting all the people there. There are so, so many children left orphans and so many mothers left widows. And some don't even know if their husbands are alive or not. They are starving, they are terrified, and they need You desperately. God of miracles, touch them. Show them that they are not alone and they already have Your love. Please!

And now, I pray for the enemy. You died for the terrorists too. It's hard to pray for them but please show them that what they are doing is wrong, it does not bring them honor or a better after-life. Reveal how they are affecting the lives of families and especially children. And Joseph Kony. I don't even like to say his name. But he is one of the leaders and a man of influence, a man that does horrific things. Maybe, God, save him so his influence can save others.

Then, Lord, I pray for my parents. It seems like they're always stressed out. With the office and the cattle, the stress doesn't stop.

Next my prayer follows the example of George Mueller by choosing 3 people to pray for, for their salvation, all the time.

Tara—She and her family are Hindu.

Sarah—Please show her that she is beautiful and You want her forever and please prevent the worst influences from taking over her.

Macie—Her parents are getting a divorce and perhaps through this situation she will come to know You as Savior.

I love You. In Your powerful name, Amen.

6-15-12

I have been reading through Proverbs and have been writing down on flash cards one verse per chapter that stands out to me. After I finish Proverbs I'll have 31 favorite verses written out. It'll be fun to go back and see which ones stood out to me before and compare to which ones will stand out later.

6-16-12

I will not be moved,

I'll say of the Lord- You are my Shield,

my Strength, my Portion, my Deliverer,

my Shelter, Strong Tower, my very present Help in time of need.

Lord, I'm in need.

I'm in need.

"Make Me Glad" by Miriam Webber

6-24-12

Guest Speaker; Missionary from Russia

Sermon Notes:

The freedom of Christianity is so great in America and is so horribly taken for granted here. Living a Christian life is not to be lived in a recliner, but on the battle field.

7-1-12

God, Yahweh,

I praise You so, so much for allowing me to go to dance camp this year. It was like going on a week long retreat with You. There was so much I got out of camp, I feel like I've grown closer to You. One thing I want to remember is, "Cars run on gasoline, we run on Jesus."

I met Tom, the only man dancing there this week. He was my prayer partner along with Caroline. He blessed me so much this week. He prayed for me the whole week. And You planned it that way to teach me that worship comes in many forms and worship through dance is not only for girls.

Creative worship was so awesome, God! You were there, working in the hearts of all those present. As we listened to the music and just sat in prayer, You began to stir hearts. Some started dancing. Some washed other's feet. Some wrote in their journals. Everybody cried. Tears of brokenness being healed. Tears of repentance, of sin being washed away. And many, many, tears of worship because You are so good. The hardest part for me was seeing all the aching and hurting people and not being able to do anything for them. Especially my closest friends hurting and I couldn't do anything. I entrust them to You forever.

Guest missionaries came and spoke. It was really good.

And You also used our dance song to teach us this week. 'When the Tears Fall' by Tim Hughes. With all the fires going on in Colorado right now and the 32,000 something people without homes to live in anymore, and again not being able to do anything for them is awful. There is a line in the song that says, 'When the storm, darkness, tears come, STILL I will praise You. Still I will sing.' It's true. And I will. But thank You, a thousand times, for such a godly family and always keeping us safe.

We leave for Illinois next week, and it's been a bad week at the office. And we had the train tickets to pay for. We didn't know how we were going to pay for them. Thank You for Your provision! Grandpa is so excited that we are coming he wants to pay for the tickets! Mama said she knows You are wanting us to go back to be lights to them. Now I know too. But I pray for our protection and please give each of us enough strength to handle the very different environment there. Especially Noah and the girls. "If Yahweh is with us, who can ever stop us?"

7-2-12

Jehovah Shalom,

My dance teacher Miss Miranda leaves today for the World Race. Eleven months of following Your voice not knowing what You will say. She knows You have called her and she is being obedient. Please calm her fears. Give her peace. Do not let the enemy break through to her. I cannot imagine the fear, the lies of the enemy, during this trip. But You will be with her and You will always be her Shield.

In Jesus, the Messiah's name, Amen.

7-4-12

Father,

Today is Independence day. We are having the Headricks over and we're going to the property early to take care of a sick cow. The Headricks are friends that are more like family. Us kids have grown up together.

God, I want to thank You for giving us freedom from sin.

Isaiah 61:1 "You gave freedom to captives, and liberty to prisoners."

Romans 8:21 "That the creation itself also be set free from its slavery to corruption into freedom of the glory of the children of God.

Galatians 5:13 "For you were called to freedom, brethren; only do not turn your freedom into an opportunity for the flesh, but through love serve one another."

1 Peter 2:16-17 "Act as free men, do not use your freedom as a covering for evil, but use it as bond-slaves of God. Honor all people, love the brotherhood, fear God, honor the king." In our case, the President.

We are free from sin forevermore! Hallelujah! Lord, this country was pronounced 'no longer a

Christian nation'. It's heartbreaking. Thank You
so much for the freedom to practice our religion
openly, without the fear of being persecuted and arrested. And I am sorry that the people of this nation
have turned their backs to You.

Jesus, I love You and trust You. Amen.

7-7-12

Today was a busy day. I was at the Dolen's early
this morning to stay with Marta (who came last
night) while the Dolen's had to go to an appointment. Marta was a Spanish exchange student visiting
a family from our church over the summer. She and
I became good friends. First, I fell asleep on the
couch for an hour! Then I got Marta up, she was
so tired with jet-lag and the traveling (it took 24
hours). We had a very, very nice day catching up.

When the Dolen's came home Marta came with
them to take me home and when we got here my
family was in the car leaving the driveway! So, I
jumped out and switched cars and we barely made it
in time for our little friend's baptism. Hallelujah!

The baptism service was good. And the point-
awesome!

Exodus 14

"God, why is this happening!? There's a sea on
this side and an army on the other…!"

"Do you trust Me?"

"But where can I go?"

"DO YOU TRUST ME?"

It was a great service.

Lord, thank You for this day. And I pray for an even better one tomorrow.

7-11-12

God,

You are Yahweh, the Unspeakable Name with power enough to whisper galaxies into orbit.

I am having a hard time describing my thoughts. I do not feel as filled up as I did after dance camp. You promised that Your Spirit would be with me and prepare me to deflect every arrow from the enemy bow. Please help me, don't let these attitudes rub off on me. Or on my fellow believers which are my physical as well as my spiritual brother, sisters and Mama (Matthew 12:50). And Daddy is all by himself this week. Please give him a good word directly from Yourself as You said in Proverbs 12:25.

Thank You for encouraging me through Hebrews 2. All of it is so powerful and touching. Verses 9-13 and 18 are the most encouraging to me. In the Name of my Savior Jesus, Amen.

7-17-12

Lord,

I love saying that. Lord.

Marta called me today. She said (imagine her beautiful Spanish accent), "You know how I hate to phone people? But I say to me, 'Marta, you must call

Maddie and say, how is your trip?' And you have to hear her voice and say 'I will see you Sunday.'" I love her.

Still, I ask for the salvation of Tara and Sarah and Macie and I add Cammy to my specifics list. She was the lady working on the train. You might call her the hostess. I gave her a tract, 'The Gospel of John' I had in my purse. She looked like she wanted to give me a hug. When she read the cover (aloud) she sounded like she had never heard of it before. She said, "Thanks so much, babe. I can't read it now but I promise I will. Thank you so much." I believe she will read it. And I pray and ask, PLEASE reveal Yourself and the truth of Your sacrifice, love and redemption to her while she reads it. I love her because You love her and I ask You to change her life.

In the Name of the Father, Son and Holy Spirit, Amen.

7-22-12

There was a theater shooting 3 days ago. Seventy-one people were shot.

Sermon notes:

It is no small thing that the tragedy happened. And it is no small thing those made in His image have their life snuffed out from under them. And it is no small thing that the God of the universe conquered it all long ago.

God is good, all the time. He is faithful always.

Exodus 33:12

You are accountable for your sins. If you are not washed in the blood of Christ, you will pay for your sin.

The devil, the slanderer, he will do all in his power to deceive you and all who were made in God's image. It is impossible for any truth to be in him.

The shooting that took place was under the influence of evil. The question: "Why would a loving God cause this to happen?"

The truth: "He wouldn't. But He allowed it to happen so that the church will do what it is supposed to do. To encourage, to counsel, to reach out."

Galatians 5:16-26 We have to live by the Spirit. "If we live by the Spirit, let us also walk by the Spirit."

7-27-12

Lord,

"Your love is unfathomable." I said this 2 days ago then asked, "Lord, how much do You love me?"

I listened for Your answer. While waiting on my knees, I felt Your hand on my head and heard Your reply, "I love you enough to call you My Own."

Thank You for loving me, mistakes and all, with an unconditional and incomprehensible love.

I remember another time shortly before this, I had my eyes closed and I asked God, "What do You see when You see me?" I immediately saw a picture of a rose in my mind and heard, "This is how I see you. You are the rose, slowly blooming into royal beauty. And this is Me, the stem. You are resting on Me and relying on Me to nurture you and grow you in a heavenward direction, and keep you tall."

Praise the Lord! My soul, my soul must sing! Beautiful Lord!

8-2-12

What do I want to be according to Your Word? Help me to be this way.

Athlete (run the race)

Bold

Cautious, Childlike

Diligent

Excellent, Example

Flexible, Faithful, Forgiving, Firm

Gentle, Generous

Humble, Honoring, Honest

Immovable

Just

Kind

Light

Mindful, Meek

Noble, Not afraid to speak, Not be moved

Obedient

Pure, Passionate, Prayerful, Patient

Quiet

Reflective, Religious in the sight of God

(James 1:27)

Servant, Shine, Strong, Slow to speak and slow to anger

Thoughtful, Truthful

Understanding

Vessel

Wise, Warrior, Without doubt

Xtremely willing

Yours

Zealous

8-3-12

Father God,

Lately I have been really wanting to do various things in Your name. But I don't know. I want to do these things but don't know if I ever can.

1. I want to go to Europe (Spain) and be an English language teacher through the Bible, as the English reference material.

2. Work with Samaritan's Purse to distribute shoeboxes, disaster relief, forest fire clean up. Local service. Oh, and by the way, our Samaritan's Purse fire clean-up day was cancelled. Too many volunteers for that day. I cried. So instead, I'm collecting donations for the church collection centers.

3. The strongest of my wishes now, at this time, is to go to a Colorado orphanage and volunteer in any way I can. Cleaning, cooking, playing games, collecting donations, whatever is needed.

Lord, All Powerful God, please arrange a way for me to do this. I think You are asking me to, so, I'm willing. The only thing I worry about is Mom and Dad. Will they let me go? Please, please arrange a way. If You want it to happen it will. In Jesus, my Savior, Your Son's name, Amen, let it be so. I trust You.

8-5-12

Sermon Notes:

The Word of God is a cup of cold water at the end of a hard day.

8-8-12

Lord,

Thank You for protecting me by not being famous. I now see that I do not want to make a difference in the world, to 'make my mark'. I want You to.

Change the world and use me, as a tool. And build a foundation, Cornerstone included, for others to rest upon. That is You and Your Word.

In Jesus' name, Amen.

8-12-12

Lord,

You are my Father. You love me enough to call me Your own. I trust You.

Mama's surgery is tomorrow. She's only having her tonsils out but still, it's a surgery. This will be an interesting, learning, exhausting, and wearing week on us all but You are still faithful and will help us all through it. Especially Mama and Daddy. He's worried. He's anxious about work and paying for the surgery. And, Mama doesn't 'do sick' very well. So this recovery is going to be difficult for her. Please, Jehovah Rapha, let this heal the pain in her throat.

Hallelujah! Party! Sing and rejoice! We went to Caroline's baptism today. Lord, You were there. I can't imagine Your happiness, when even mine is as strong as it is, when we watched so many people publicly profess their faith. Hallelujah, Lord!

8-13-12

Jehovah Shalom,

I have felt so emotional today. But I suppose it was bottled up most of the day and is only now just coming out.

I almost fainted at the hospital. I almost cried there too after seeing Mama hurting after the surgery. And seeing Daddy caress, comfort and tend to her. I had a tiny glimpse of what its like to feel the pain of someone you love so much, I could hardly look. You watched Your Son die, and had to look away. Thank You for looking away. I may be the first to thank You for that but I humbly and earnestly mean it.

Daddy is really stressed. He was smiling a bit more tonight, but for me, it hurts to see it. It's almost like he's trying to hide it for our sake. And I can't do anything. Please relieve his anxieties, Lord.

Give him a 'good word to make his heart glad', like Proverbs 12:25 says.

Thank You for helping me feel so willing and patient to serve my family. Please continue helping me feel selfless in my service to my family.

In Jesus' name I trust, Amen.

8-20-12

Lord,

You have blessed me through Mama again. She came to get me up last weekend and she said, 'There she is. She shines almost as bright as her Savior.'

And later I was telling her how much You have blessed me by giving me to her, and she said, 'I am so glad God is sharing you with me.'

Thank You a thousand times over for Mama. And the rest of my family. But still, I'd rather be shared by You and live for You than for anyone else.

8-21-12

Lord,

I've been thinking this all day and I have to write it down. All of those coats that I cleaned out of my closet (lots and lots of them) I am giving them to You. They have Your name on them. So, I gave the bag of Your coats to a friend because she knows some people who need coats now that it's starting to get cold. Please use them to further Your Kingdom and spread Your love. It breaks Your heart to see Your children cold when, I have too many coats just for me. Please warm them with Your love, and Your coats. In Jesus' name, Amen.

9-3-12

Lord,

This has been such a crazy weekend. Daddy has been off work since Thursday, so, we have been working at the ranch 5 days in a row now. Except Sunday, we just fed the cattle and came home. No big projects. But Noah and Briggham camped out there on Saturday night. Morgan and I camped that night in the tree house. It was so fun! There were a lot of coyotes out that night. We tried swimming in the pond, but then we saw 3 snakes all by the water. Just little ones but we decided not to swim. On Sunday Briggham led church at the property for us. It was so good.

Sermon notes: Philippians 2

Be humble.

How? Obedience. Respect. Honor your parents. Do not argue or complain.

Who? All who love Christ will want to do His work.

Why? We will shine like stars.

Thank You, Lord, for using Brigg to teach me. I got more out of this service than I have in a service for a while. I love You and will obey You.

Today though, Lord, was tough. You truly do give exactly what we need for each situation when we are willing to receive the gifts You have to offer us. Everything was just irritating as soon as I woke up.

At the ranch we tried to draw blood from the cows (for preg testing) and it was discouraging because it wasn't working. Daddy was frustrated and really stressed out. I was helping him and told him that I was going to get him a fresh, not bloody, paper towel for the next try to draw blood. He told me not to mouth him. I didn't think that I did. It didn't sound like it to me. It really hurt. He's so stressed.

All day I had been talking with You to help me. But You were teaching me how sometimes our efforts are not appreciated. Then I was talking with You and crying and listening to the song "I am" by Jill Philips. You definitely spoke to me at the words 'Drop your burden, Mine is light.' I had to ask, "Jesus, what is Your burden?"

I reflected on what Your life here on earth looked like and what did I see? Forget yourself. Serve others.

That is Your burden. It is very light. And today You reminded me that I am keeping one hand open for whatever You drop into it, but You have my other hand in Your own. I don't have words to express my gratitude and love for You.

In Your indescribable Name, Amen.

9-7-12

Father,

Last night our small group started a Kay Arthur study about prayer. It is very good so far. We are looking at the prayers in the Old Testament.

There is one thing I don't understand. Someone mentioned praying for your enemies and someone else reminded us that in the Old Testament a lot of the prayers were 'crush the enemy' and 'give us victory'. Not 'let them see their wrong and repent'.

I have been praying for Joseph Kony in Africa. A Muslim leader who is responsible for a lot of the horrific, awful things they're doing right now. Maybe he isn't to be saved. Nothing seems to be happening so, crush him, Lord. Deliver Your children out of his hand. Yet, in this case, it goes deeper. A spiritual battle which You have already won. You have defeated the enemy forever! Hallelujah!

One thing I heard You say as I was praying was, Ecclesiastes 3:3 "A time to kill, and a time to heal. A time to tear down, and a time to build. There is an appointed time for everything, for every event under the sun."

9-9-12

Church notes while camping with Diana.

Mark 3 - The Maddie paraphrase

Verse 2: They were watching Jesus to accuse Him. The same way the enemy watches us and waits for when we falter in our weaknesses.

Verse 4: The Pharisees were so concerned about the rules that they didn't see the sick man as they should have. Jesus reminded them, "Who would leave his neighbor's sheep to die on the Sabbath? Yet not even look with pity and love on this man? So, why would healing this man, saving his life, on the Sabbath be wrong?"

Verse 5: They are so angry with Jesus that they don't see any good. We need to be very careful and not think ill of someone because of their faults. Don't harden your hearts toward them. Ask the Holy Spirit to open our eyes to see His view of that person.

Matthew 12:12, "How much more valuable is a man than a sheep! So yes, it is lawful to do good on the Sabbath."

9-11-12

Today Lord, I came home from staying with the Wanright family. Mr. and Mrs. Wanright were in the mountains on a retreat and asked if I could stay the night with their kids. It was SO fun! I am so, so impressed with their laid back attitudes and just the way their house operates. We went on a fly hunt. But their only two fly-swatters were ripped and falling apart, so we taped them and had two people follow the swatters with brooms. We lost count after 35 flies.

My favorite part was playing dodge ball on their patio. Prison dodge ball. Which is the best. It was two of the boys versus everyone else. So, two against six. They won most of the time. All dozen or so kick balls were flat, torn or shredded, but we used them anyway. And it was a blast! Even the little four year old did pretty good.

Yesterday, there was a field trip at Glen Eyre Castle in Colorado Springs to see the Dead Sea Scrolls exhibit. I learned so much and was awesruck at how incredible You are. The scrolls themselves were found by a twelve year old shepherd boy looking for his goat. Isaiah is the only book that was found complete, without pieces missing. And only the Old Testament was written on them. And, I didn't know this, the Torah (the first 5 books of the Old Testament), even today is forbidden to be written with vowels. For clarity in what the passage is saying. The example he gave us was, "If the passage says 'shv yr brds' you would clearly understand that you shave your beards not your brides."

The parchments were sheep hide sewn together by tendons. And to decipher the scrolls, scientists used infrared light to see the differences in handwriting and find the DNA on the material. Every one of the scrolls match the Old Testament perfectly, not even one spelling error! AND we got to hold and look through a 400 year old original King James Bible. It was so exciting! And the castle was so beautiful. And today, through Your faithfulness, You have provided rain. Real rain, not just a mist. It's supposed to continue through evening. You are so amazing. I love You.

9-12-12

God,

I'm scared. I had the best last two days, then this morning, the American Ambassador in Libya was killed. That's how WWII started. You say, "Fear not, I am with you always." And I know that, God. But please, come quickly! Your people need Your presence, especially in the Middle East.

I can hear You say, "Be still, my child. I know, I know. Now, you need to know that I am God."

You are Yahweh, the All Knowing, and All Seeing One. You hear the prayers of those who are seeking refuge. Show them that You are near. Be their shield and where they can rest their head. (Psalm 3:3)

On a lighter note… tonight Claire and I were in Mom and Dad's room and Morgan was on the floor. Claire wanted me to rub her back. I did and said, "Claire, you've got a bubble butt just like the rest of us."

She gasps, "Maddie!" And laughs at the same time.

From the floor Morgan says, "I don't have a bubble butt."

Claire and I at the same time, "Oh yes you do!"

Oh my gosh, I laughed so hard.

9-13-12

God,

Yesterday at Bible study I came to realize, I'm not treating Noah right as a sister.

I tell him that I don't expect much from him.

1 Corinthians 13:5 "Love is not rude."

I don't want to listen to his reasoning.

1 Corinthians 13:4 "Love is patient."

I let my tongue run off when I am angry.

Ephesians 4:29 "Let no unwholesome word proceed from your mouth but only such a word as is good for the edification according to the need of the moment, so that it will give grace to all who hear."

I don't say 'I love you' or 'I appreciate that' or 'you're a great brother'.

John 13:34 "Love one another. As I have loved you."

Please forgive my many mistakes. Shape me, God. Shape me into the encouraging sister You need me to be.

9-17-12

Jehovah of so many names, I love You!

A few days ago, we were visiting with our new neighbors the McGavery's when Mama asked what church they go to. Mrs. McGavery hesitated and responded, "We belong to the church of the Latter Day Saints."

But as I reflect on what she said I am struck by how she didn't say, 'Oh, such and such church in Elizabeth' or whatever, but just 'our church'. As a body, a whole. That is exactly the way Your church should be, God. And it saddens me that we don't often enough refer to ourselves as the body of Christ. We are not in unity. We just say, "I'm Presbyterian, Methodist, Non-denominational." It is not, "I belong to the body of Jesus Christ."

Father, please, please, help us all reflect You to unbelievers by our unity.

In Jesus' name, Amen.

9-20-12

Lord,

We're studying Esther in Precept studies now and I wondered, "What's my 'such a time as this'?" Let me see why I am here for such a time as this.

9-23-12

Sermon notes:

He is faithful and has purchased me.

"I am your shield and will deflect the blows of the enemy. I am your shield and buckler, you can do all things through Me. Of course I want you! I bought you! Of course I want to spend time with you. So, come spend time with Me."

God takes care of His own. How much more does He care for you than the birds, flowers or sheep?

9-30-12

Sermon notes:

Fish are made to be in water, we are made to be in God's presence.

Mark 3:13 "And He went up on the mountain and summoned those whom He Himself wanted, and they came to Him."

Jesus took time to climb up the mountain to spend time with His Father. Likewise we need to make time to enjoy His presence.

Note from Jesus:

WANTED
World Changers
No experience necessary
Perfection not required

10-3-12

Father,

I love saying Your name. Thank You for adopting me. Me, so willingly.

This last week I asked You to show me how to obey. Now I see that the task before me is servant-hood. For now, anyway, You have asked me to serve by placing me in such a time as this, to serve all who are around me. My family, friends, neighbors, and the random guy at the store.

This morning, Lord, I was feasting on the Living Bread. I saw in Exodus 5, You promised Moses that You would teach him what to say. Would You teach me what to "say what is good for edification of the moment, so that it gives grace to those who hear"? While serving I want to be able to speak grace.

Please be with my mouth, and teach me to speak.
Thank You Holy Spirit.

Ephesians 3:20 "Him who is able to do far more
abundantly beyond all that we ask or think, according to the power that works within us."

10-8-12

Father,

I am very grateful that I am not a cow. Because,
I don't want to live outside in the cold. On Friday,
Lord, I had the best day! It snowed and just Dad
and I went out to the ranch. Not only did I get
7 hours of work in that day and was freezing and
shaking from the cold most of the day, I could tell
that Daddy was tense and stressed all day but I didn't
mind. Lord, You made me feel so laid back! A few
times I found myself just riding along or working or
helping Dad but I didn't know what we were doing
or what the plan was and I didn't mind! Your burden
is indeed very light. It was the best day, God. Please,
please allow me to be laid back in a humble attitude
of service all of this week. Thank You, Father.

XO, Amen

10-10-12

Father,

Now that it's Christmas time, Operation Christmas Child is a big thing that has lit up my fire and
this year I am blessed by having the opportunity to
serve at the warehouse 3 times. And I want to vol-

unteer at Southeast Christian Church during their packing party.

I wanted to keep this Fall open for anything You need me to do, or anywhere You wanted me to go. But I'm pretty sure You have stationed me here in my own mission field in Colorado. And if Your timing for me hasn't come, then please, let my heart understand. I trust You.

10-14-12

Oh Lord,

The last few days have been tough. Thursday, we were all packing for vacation in Pagosa Springs and everyone was gone and I was so stressed and I couldn't handle the loads of stuff I had to do. Well, I was freaking out when Mama got home and I was yelling… she said she hasn't heard me talk like that in a long, long time. It was an encouragement and a compliment to hear, though I'm sad that I was yelling in the first place.

Thank You so much for the grace You have given me and taught me to live by. Please, continue teaching me. I am grateful for my shortcomings because they remind me of how great You are and keeps me in check.

Friday, Lord, was hard. We were all ready to leave for vacation. We were all loaded in Mom's car and there was something wrong with the car. Dad said if the problem was what he thought it was, we could get stranded halfway to Pagosa.

By the way, when we got back from Pagosa and took the car in, the strange sound we heard was only a rock clicking and bumping around somewhere in the undercarriage. So, we could have taken the car anyway but no, we all crammed into Dad's truck.

So, we hurry and get Dad's truck ready to go. Vacuumed and windows washed, and finally all loaded up to leave. On top of the quick change of plans, and all six of us squished in Dad's truck, my tummy hurt so bad that day. It was not good. We were gonna meet the Stevens' at the Sand Dunes and hike around there since its halfway to Pagosa anyway.

The dunes were great, though. It was nothing like I expected trekking through the desert to be, cold, windy, and it started to hail, and rain, and lightning. It was still a highlight of our trip, though. When we finished our six hour drive we all watched 'Wipeout' until midnight. That's a funny show. We don't have TV reception at home so when we're on vacation, that's what we watch. Boy, do I hate all those stupid, disrespectful, trashy commercials.

Yesterday (Saturday), Dad said I was really grumpy (for the third day). I didn't feel like I was, though. We didn't do much of anything. It was so nice.

Today, I got up early to do Day 1, Lesson 2 of

Leviticus in our Precept Bible study. Thank You for Jesus' willing sacrifice for my atonement.

Mama bought sausages for breakfast this morning, and I only ate three. Then I felt so sick I thought I would cry. Mom and Dad were at a meeting all morning, and the majority of the time that they were gone I spent in the bathroom. I tried everything to try to feel better. I took a bath. Nope, didn't help. Sleep it off. Nope. Finally I just threw up and felt better. Stupid sausages.

We went for a walk, went to lunch, then went shopping in the only stores that were open, which were all antique shops. I stayed in the car for some of them and took a nap. I'm so grateful that Mom and Dad weren't there this morning to worry over my ickyness.

After we got back, we played mini golf and went swimming. It was a wonderful afternoon. Oh my word, it was so funny! You know how Morgan obsesses about her watch and she barely takes it off and nobody is supposed to touch it? Well, we were playing mini golf and there were sections of the course that were under the shade of some trees. We were in the middle of a game when Mama starts laughing so hard she can't even speak. So, we don't know what she's laughing at. Then, Morgan is frozen with one arm extended. Her face is red and she looks terrified and livid at the same time. We all look at her hand and lo and behold a bird had pooped right on her watch! We all were laughing so hard we couldn't breathe. Morgan got so mad. But really though, it was one of the funniest things I've ever seen.

I have once again come to the realization that my family, and my own body, are very healthy. Thank You for our health. And thank You that we don't get sick very often. I love You, Lord

10-15-12

Jeremiah 17:7-10

"Blessed is the man who trusts in the Lord. For he will be like a tree planted by the water, that extends its roots by a stream and will not fear when the heat comes; but its leaves will be green, and it will not be anxious of the drought not cease to yield fruit.

The heart is deceitful above all else and desperately sick, who can understand it?

I, the Lord, search the heart, I test the mind, even to give to each man according to the results of his deeds."

What kind of fruit do I produce? Do I fear the heat or storms or drought?

Father,

I caught that kiss You blew to me today. And the power of the love that it carried has not faded.

Today, at Treasure Falls, seeing how beautiful You made it for me to see was indescribable. The water dancing at the top was proof that nature praises You. And the rainbows waving in the mist made me feel like I could touch a promise. It was one of the most beautiful things I have ever seen.

10-16-12

Wow. God, today was amazing! We went to Mesa Verde to see the ancient cliff dwellings. There were over 40 dwellings and we were told you couldn't throw a cat without hitting a dwelling of some kind.

Cliff Palace was breathtaking. So was the Balcony House. Eight hundred year old structures still standing with so much history but so much more mystery. The rangers kept referring to them as the 'stone age'. But clearly, the cliff dwellers were very intelligent.

Pueblo Indians inhabited the mesa tops for years. Planting corn, beans, and squash, then finally decided to build in the cliffs. Their geometry and architectural skills blow me away. They had an obsession with right angles. Fireplaces were everywhere, a room was an average 6 by 8 feet in diameter. The average person size was 5 foot to 5 foot 4 inches, mostly due to malnutrition. They used sandstone to grind their corn, but the sand got in their food and eroded their teeth. We saw handprints, footprints, and fingerprints in the clay. Sandstone, and juniper trees were used in all their architecture. They moved out of the cliff dwellings in roughly 1200AD.

The most amazing thing, though, was their religion. You, Lord, really did set eternity in their hearts. The Indians knew that this was not their home, that there is more than just this life. They knew they could ask for rain and would be provided for but didn't know that it was You. They knew that there was a creation. You set eternity in the hearts of those people, and their descendants are still here today! Please use their traditions to lead them to You and the truth You have to offer.

Thank You, Father for this gift of us being able to explore and learn about these people 800 years later. So we can see Your greatness, because You are the same yesterday, today and forever. And You are bigger than any of these things and bigger than history itself.

Thank You, thank You, thank You, Amen.

10-20-12

Sermon notes:

Ecclesiastes 8:12 "Still I know that it will be well with those who fear God, who fear Him openly."

1 Thessalonians 3:4 "For indeed while we were still with you, we kept telling you in advance that we were going to suffer affliction."

Always obeying Jesus will cause friction and trouble. But you will always win and come out on top when He is in charge and when you allow Him to be Lord.

10-22-12

Lord Almighty,

This is a scary time, there have been so many child abductions and attempted abductions just in the last few weeks. At least three in Colorado.

Thank You for Your protection for us and those around us.

Since it is October, I think the abductions are for the wicca. One in a hundred kidnappings are. And the 31st is a night when they do something. I don't know what, but I know that the followers of wicca do something. God, darkness flees when light is present. Colorado isn't very bright. The evil in this ever present darkness is not welcome. Scripture says this sort of thing will be around the end of the age. So, come quickly Lord! And please get that kidnapper caught. In Jesus' name.

Prayer answered on the 23rd. Suspect was arrested.

10-26-12

God,

Yesterday at Bible study Mrs. Lewis said something I want to make a part of my life. I want to give you my day then say, "Okay, Boss, what do You have on my schedule today?" Don't be annoyed at every interruption, it's an appointment set by God, Boss of your day, don't miss it!

I am reading 'Jonathan's Journey' right now and the part when Jesus makes the little girl is the sweetest part yet. I love what she says,

"You made me for Yourself, and I will be grateful to You forever! My heart is entirely Yours and I long to serve You! What might I do to please You best?"

That's my prayer, Lord, and I love You so much! Amen.

P.S. Thank You for the beautiful snow.

10-28-12

Sermon notes:

Five finger prayers. There was a man who needed the Lord but didn't know where to begin. So a Christian buddy of his told him to start with this prayer everyday for one week. One word per finger.

Lord, Please Show Me Myself.

At the end of that week the man was a mess. He felt wretched. The Lord had indeed shown the man who he was and he didn't like what he saw in himself. So then the buddy told him another prayer to pray everyday for the next week.

Lord, Please Show Me Yourself.

And it changed his life forever.

The heart of God is for missionaries. He wants every tongue, tribe and nation to know Him. He Himself is a missionary. So, if He sends missionaries out, then He went out there first. He is already where He leads you.

11-1-12

Oh Father,

Yesterday I gave my day to You and every interruption was an appointment. I'm going along in my schoolwork and Claire comes bursting into my room, "Maddie! We're going to the 'Little Princess' play and Mom forgot and it starts in 5 minutes, so we gotta go!"

I'm thinking, "Okay… that's a fun appointment, Lord."

The play was great but during it I was thinking that I didn't understand why that was an appointment. At the end we were all walking out and we ran into an old friend we hadn't seen in ages! Now I see what Your appointment was for me! We got to catch up a little bit and she was just as excited to see us as we were to see her! I pray for her now, Lord. Please, don't allow her to be influenced by the world and protect her from its allurement. If it was Your time for me to become friends with her again, then I'm ready. Please don't allow me to put my guard down just because of who it is. Her life has changed. My life has changed. Strengthen me for whatever lies ahead.

And please protect Dad and Noah on their hunting trip this weekend. And give peace to Mama while they're gone.

11-4-12

Sermon notes:

Jesus already came as a lamb. Next time, He's coming as a lion!

11-6-12

8:15pm Election Day.

Lord, I'm here on my knees asking You to allow our country to stand. Right now the numbers and tallies are making us sick. There are many who have

125

lied when voting, cheated while voting, and stolen votes for this election. But no matter the outcome, You are King. I trust You entirely.

I am reading Isaiah right now and I came across Isaiah 38:19, "It is the living, who give thanks to You, as I do today. A father tells his sons of Your faithfulness."

You will always be faithful. To the end.

Whoever is elected, thank You that it'll only be for four years, but please provide comfort and peace no matter what happens. In Jesus' name, Amen.

11-7-12

Apparently Lord, You have different plans for our country than any of us expected. Well, of course, You will provide for us. I am having a very hard time accepting this part of Your plan. Help me. I keep telling myself, "The sun will still rise and fall as it has before and the seasons will still come and go." But money will be much harder to come by. Teach me to spend wisely.

I worry about Mama and Daddy though. I trust You with them too.

Isaiah 42:10,13 "Sing to the Lord a new song, sing His praise from the end of the earth! You who go down to the sea, and all that is in it. You islands, and those who dwell on them.

The Lord will go forth like a warrior, He will arouse His zeal like a man of war. He will utter a shout, yes, He will raise a war cry. He will prevail against His enemies."

11-18-12

This week Father, You opened my eyes. You gave me my first experience we've been preparing for in Worldview.

Hannah and Caroline and I were at Barnes and Noble. While browsing through the Christian literature section we heard two girls arguing while looking through a Bible. "'Made them in our image, male and female.' So, there must be two gods. A mother god and a father God."

We couldn't just stand there! So we asked if we could explain it to them. We explained that, no, there is only the Father God. No mother god. And He made man in His Image through Jesus Christ, John 1:1. Then they started arguing with us too. I know You were there but it was eye opening for us. We are not aware of all that is out there. Thank You for the experience and please open the eyes of those girls so they can see the flaw in their reasoning, and lead them to truth.

11-20-12

Father,

The dance recital last night was so powerful! I know You did great things in so many hearts, God. The whole theme was Your faithfulness, and You are faithful! Always! Never once have You failed.

They showed a video of all the dance students with a summary of their testimonies. They each had a paper or cardboard sign that had a word to describe how they saw themselves before Jesus. And the next picture is the sign flipped over with a word that describes how the Lord sees them.

Even though I wasn't dancing I want to make a sign too. My side would be, "I feel so Useless."

But Jesus sees me as, "Full of Purpose. Strategically placed for such a time as this."

You are faithful, even when I am not. We don't praise God because life is good. We praise Him because He is good!

11-27-12

Father,

I'm reading 1 Corinthians now and I feel You speaking to me,

1 Corinthians 6:13-20, "Yet the body is not for immorality but for the Lord and the Lord is for the body... the immoral person sins against their own body. Your body is a temple for the Holy Spirit and you are not your own... you were bought with a price, therefore glorify God in your body."

I want this to be me. 1 Corinthians 7:34 "The young lady, is concerned about the holy things of the Lord, that she may be holy in both body and spirit. This I say to you for your own benefit; not to put a restraint upon you but to promote what is appropriate and to secure undistracted devotion to the Lord."

God, let's elope. I want to be married to You, Lord, and maybe eventually we can add a husband into our relationship and the three of us will grow closer together. Like the triangle image with You at the top and me and him at the bottom, and the only way to grow closer together is to grow closer to You too. Show me how to live like I need to when I belong to You. Amen.

12-1-12

Wise men still seek Him.

12-2-12

Sermon notes:

Christianity is the only religion that addresses sin.

We were slaves to sin, but there is GOOD NEWS! we are REDEEMED!

We are Yours and Yours forever. We cannot be traded or sold. BECAUSE WE ARE TREASURED!

12-4-12

I see Your faithfulness. Father, the night before last I was feeling really crummy about myself. Asking, "What am I worth? What good am I doing? Why do I say things that come out all wrong then get in trouble for it?" And then, You told me, "You are worth more than My life. I see a treasure when I look at you." Whoa.

At church they talked about how laughter will turn to mourning over sin. In order for comfort to come, mourning has to come. That's what I'm doing, mourning for my sin.

Last night we went to another dance recital with the theme: "God is Faithful." It is so true! While we were there You opened my eyes and pricked my memory. Oh yeah, I asked You to show me myself didn't I? Well, You did and I realized that I have nothing to offer You except what You've already given me. You pursue me every day and I want to see it! Now that You've shown me myself, Father, show me Yourself.

12-10-12

God,

I praise You for the snow outside right now that we've been praying for. You are so faithful.

Looking through my Bible study, I think about the Israelites. You kept telling them, "Did you already forget that I brought you out of this? I'm capable to do it again if you trust Me."

Same for my family. You brought us out of a rough time before. Forgive our lack of faith. Please strengthen our faith. You have never let us down before, why would You now? Because You wouldn't. Ever!

Thank You for Your faithfulness and Your provision. And for speaking to me today.

P.S. God, send Daddy a kiss today, and make it obvious it's from You. Please. In Jesus' name.

12-17-12

God, my tongue is untamable. I feel like sending

it away until it can speak words helpful in the moment not tearing down and discouraging and getting into trouble. I want to hate my tongue! As I look back at my other journal entries I see me asking You to teach me to speak and to take my mind and train it to control the tongue. I remember begging You to burn the old Maddie so I can't ever get her back and I remind myself, "That's something the old Maddie would do, or say, that shouldn't be there. You took that out a long time ago." I don't want any of it back!

Take the dirty impurities and sin out of my heart and wash it clean. Bleach it or clean it out or completely remodel if You have to. I don't want my mouth hurting others any more.

And I have decided as of now, I am no longer thinking of myself as the old Maddie. And no longer getting angry as the old Maddie often did. But I can't do it alone.

I love my family too much to hurt them.

In Jesus' name I beg You. Amen.

12-28-12

For daily bread, for all things good,
for life and health, for this our food,
for each good gift, Your grace and power,
we thank Thee Lord with humble hearts.
Amen

New Years Eve 2012

God, I praise You for another year of learning about You.

- In January I got my drivers license! (I thought I'd never get it!)
- This summer I attended a 'Set-Apart Girl Conference' and You taught me a lot that weekend.
- Also, in June I attended CMA dance camp! I felt You so close to me, Father! I felt You there and the Holy Spirit moved in great ways!
- We went back to Illinois a week later.
- This year You gave and took away. Katie, our dog, had her first litter of puppies! Four female, one male. And Noah kept one, Hazel, but old Meg had to be put down. We had 11 years with her. Thank You. And we had our first calving season. Expected seven, and five survived.
- The Headricks moved back here from New Mexico. And perfect timing too. Noah and Mom and Dad needed some good friends to talk to and encourage them.
- President Obama was elected to his second term and all I ask is, God, come quickly!
- We picked out a cosmetology school and I start this coming fall.
- I think the latest of my exciting news is, I'm

done with chemistry!!! As of a week ago. SO GLAD!!!

- Within the last month Grandpa Otto has been doing badly and his health is going downhill. I don't know what to pray for. He might not make it much longer.

You are faithful, Lord, and looking back at this past year I see Your fingerprints all over the place!

How I did on last year's goals:

1. Be a responsible driver. Well, I haven't been pulled over yet or taken out anyone's mail-box, but I can't be over confident.

2. Start Cosmetology School and get a job. I'm working at the ranch and babysitting, but no school yet. We did pick which one though!

3. Do the middle splits. Nope. Still getting there.

4. Memorize apologetics verses from my World-view notes. Uh, embarrassed to say, no I haven't done a lot of memorizing, but I know what God says. I just need to work on where He says them.

5. Be more laid back and 'go with the flow.' I am still learning, though I am getting better. My secret is to forget myself. It works like that, *snap*.

January 1st, 2013

Father,

I humbly ask You to prepare me for everything 2013 brings. I am willing to keep one hand open if You will take the other.

MY 2013 GOALS:

1. Learn to control my tongue. To make diamonds and gems come out instead of snakes and toads.
2. I want to be a good example to those around me and shine brighter than a star.
3. I really want an A in Algebra.
4. Make my arms stronger and keep my body in a little better than just "good" shape.
5. Save money every month for school.

Afterword

And so, dear Reader, to conclude this volume, I am pleased to tell you that I have completed Cosmetology school and am in the workplace. My family still owns the ranch, though I don't work on it as often as I had in the years that you just read about. There have been ups and there have been downs, but the Lord has carried me through it all.

"I have set the Lord continually before me. Because He is at my right hand, I will not be shaken." Psalm 16:8

Have I been shaken? Yes. Have I cracked? No. Why? Because my foundation, my Cornerstone, is strong and holds me firm. He is faithful. Hold fast. Be steadfast. Offer Him every facet of every detail of your life. Give Him your heart, He will keep it safe. That doesn't mean that pain won't ever touch it, but it will be held by the ultimate Healer that will use the pain for its own purpose.

Proverbs 16:4 "For the Lord has made everything for its own purpose. Even evil for its day of judgment."

I am still learning, and growing. That won't ever stop. And I still, daily, fall even more in love with my Creator, my God, my Savior, my Lord, my Father. Let's do *today*, Lord! And this week, and this year! No matter what faces me, I'll still be Yours. I trust You. Through the ups and downs, backwards and inside-outs. Through the laughs and the tears, I will cling to You.

ACKNOWLEDGMENTS

Dearest Mrs. Lewis, thank you for encouraging me and teaching me for so many years. And for truly helping get this book rolling. You have blessed me in ways you don't even know.

The Reinhart family, for being such an amazing family and contributing to a huge chunk of this book.

Hannah and Caroline, my Sisters in Christ, thank you for always being there for me and loving me in my good and bad moments. I love you bushelfulls!

Emily and Diana Gensen. You know all the extra things we did and teased each other about in between these pages that weren't recorded. Thank you for your example and for being the ones I looked up to as older sisters.

And Kirren, my dear, sweet, quiet friend. Thank you for the years we've been friends and the memories we've had together.

To the many, many mentioned in my book, you have all impacted my life even if you didn't know it! You have taught me and mentored me and helped me grow closer to the Lord. I am forever grateful for all of you. And those whose names are perhaps not written in these pages, know that you all have your own special place in my heart. And you know what?

You are still mentoring me and teaching me. Thank you!

To my family who supported me, encouraged me, and helped me during the writing of this book. I never could have done this if you guys didn't think I could.

Mama, my best friend and mentor. Thank you for helping to smooth out the rough edges of this book, and for always being ready to hug me and pray with me and say, "We're all good." And the million other things that I can't possibly explain. I still want to be just like you someday.

Daddy, your arms have always been a safe place for me. Thank you for letting me come to you for wisdom and comfort. You have given me such a godly example and continue to guide and support me. Thank you for everything that you do.

And the siblings!

Noah, for taking such good care of us sisters and being such a good friend to me my whole life. I love the hundreds of inside jokes we have. You're awesome. I so admire you, brother.

Morgan, for being the ray of sunshine that you always are. Quiet and patient, I want you to know that I learn from you every single day. I see the Lord working in your life. You have such a radiant heart. Don't ever let anyone dim your light just because it's shining in their eyes.

Claire, the giggly spark of awesome that you are! You are growing up so fast. You are so beautiful. The Lord is going to use the fiery passion in you to do some amazing things. In fact, He already is! Don't doubt that. I love you!

You guys inspired me to write this book in the first place. Please learn from my mistakes. Don't copy mine; believe me, you'll make plenty of your own. I want you to know that I am always here for you. I am so excited to see what the Lord is going to do in your lives! I pray for you daily and love you sooo much!

And finally, to my Father, Yahweh. You are my God and You led me to write this book. It was in my handwriting, but I'm just recording Your composition of my life. You have always been faithful and You are so, so good. So, Father, may this book glorify You and You can use it any way You like. I am Yours.

Love,

Your Madison

CPSIA information can be obtained
at www.ICGtesting.com
Printed in the USA
LVOW12s0408190117
521501LV00001B/3/P

9 780997 426717